**New Directions for
Student Services**

John H. Schuh
EDITOR-IN-CHIEF

Elizabeth J. Whitt
ASSOCIATE EDITOR

e-Portfolios:
Emerging Opportunities for Student Affairs

Jeff W. Garis
Jon C. Dalton
EDITORS

Number 119 • Fall 2007
Jossey-Bass
San Francisco

E-PORTFOLIOS: EMERGING OPPORTUNITIES FOR STUDENT AFFAIRS
Jeff W. Garis, Jon C. Dalton (eds.)
New Directions for Student Services, no. 119
John H. Schuh, Editor-in-Chief
Elizabeth J. Whitt, Associate Editor

NEW DIRECTIONS FOR STUDENT SERVICES (ISSN 0164-7970, e-ISSN 1536-0695) is part of The Jossey-Bass Higher and Adult Education Series and is published quarterly by Wiley Subscription Services, Inc., A Wiley Company, at Jossey-Bass, 989 Market Street, San Francisco, California 94103-1741. Periodicals Postage Paid at San Francisco, California, and at additional mailing offices. POSTMASTER: Send address changes to New Directions for Student Services, Jossey-Bass, 989 Market Street, San Francisco, CA 94103-1741.

New Directions for Student Services is indexed in CIJE: Current Index to Journals in Education (ERIC), Contents Pages in Education (T&F), Current Abstracts (EBSCO), Education Index/Abstracts (H.W. Wilson), Educational Research Abstracts Online (T&F), ERIC Database (Education Resources Information Center), and Higher Education Abstracts (Claremont Graduate University).

Microfilm copies of issues and articles are available in 16mm and 35mm, as well as microfiche in 105mm, through University Microfilms Inc., 300 North Zeeb Road, Ann Arbor, Michigan 48106-1346.

SUBSCRIPTIONS cost $85 for individuals and $209 for institutions, agencies, and libraries in the United States. See ordering information page at end of book.

EDITORIAL CORRESPONDENCE should be sent to the Editor-in-Chief, John H. Schuh, N 243 Lagomarcino Hall, Iowa State University, Ames, Iowa 50011.

Wiley Bicentennial Logo: Richard J. Pacifico

www.josseybass.com

CONTENTS

EDITORS' NOTES

The development and application of e-portfolios within higher education are rapidly emerging at national and international levels. Their design and use are varied, ranging from e-portfolios to support the learning process through reflection, assessment-based systems that are often used in support of institutional accreditation, and so-called showcase e-portfolios, used in support of students' career development and employment.

Institutions are increasingly expressing interest in e-portfolios, but many have not developed a sufficient knowledge base and supporting model for creating and implementing a college- or university-wide system. The initiative for some higher education e-portfolios is driven by the campus technology support group, others are led by academic affairs administrators, and some e-portfolios are sponsored by student affairs. The e-portfolio system may be vendor based and supported externally, or created and maintained by institutions themselves. Some e-portfolios are student based, under their control and intended as a student service, while others are driven and controlled by the institution with the intent of providing data in support of the college or university learning mission.

The purpose of this volume, *e-Portfolios: Emerging Opportunities for Student Affairs,* is to examine the range of e-portfolio systems, consider various design considerations associated with e-portfolios, provide examples of e-portfolio models at selected institutions, and examine the importance for student affairs leadership in creating an e-portfolio delivery system. This volume places primary focus on career or showcase e-portfolios intended for student use and often involving student affairs and supporting units such as career services.

In Chapter One, Jeff W. Garis addresses the range of e-portfolio systems and provides several criteria for consideration in creating and implementing a higher education e portfolio system. He looks at sample systems and refers readers to sources for additional information.

In Chapter Two, Glenn Johnson and Jack R. Rayman describe a flexible e-portfolio system created by an academic department in cooperation with student affairs and career services at the Pennsylvania State University. The chapter addresses university-wide collaboration in creating the student-based e-portfolio.

Diane J. Goldsmith describes a statewide e-portfolio effort in Connecticut in Chapter Three. The application of e-portfolios in community colleges as well as small colleges is addressed, along with a discussion of e-portfolios as learning and assessment-based tools.

NEW DIRECTIONS FOR STUDENT SERVICES, no. 119, Fall 2007 © Wiley Periodicals, Inc.
Published online in Wiley InterScience (www.interscience.wiley.com) • DOI: 10.1002/ss.244

In Chapter Four, Jill A. Lumsden chronicles the development and implementation of the Career Portfolio at the Florida State University (FSU). She offers considerable detail in support of the this concept and design, which have been used by over forty-five thousand students since they began in 2002.

In Chapters Five and Six, career services directors and staff from student affairs units describe the implementation of an e-portfolio based on the FSU concept and design at the University of California, San Diego (UCSD) and the Georgia Institute of Technology (Georgia Tech). Andrew Ceperley and Craig Schmidt chronicle a highly successful project in implementing an e-portfolio system at UCSD, and Ralph Mobley offers a detailed discussion of the challenges associated with creating such a system at Georgia Tech.

In Chapter Seven, Robert C. Reardon and Sarah Lucas Hartley address the need for systematic approaches to evaluating the range of emerging e-portfolio systems. They offer several models of program evaluation and provide an overview of professional standards related to e-portfolios.

Jon C. Dalton closes the volume in Chapter Eight with an overview of several key issues associated with the implementation of e-portfolio systems in higher education. Also, he offers several thoughts for considering e-portfolio programs and reasserts the importance for student affairs to assume leadership roles in the institution-wide implementation of e-portfolio systems.

We hope that student affairs professionals will find this volume to be helpful in increasing their awareness and understanding of e-portfolios as well as learning about sources for additional information regarding the range of systems. We believe that e-portfolios will continue to evolve as an important learning and student support application in higher education. They will be used as tools in support of the institutional learning mission, institutional assessment and accreditation, and student career development. It will be critical for student affairs to play a key role in the implementation of e-portfolio systems in colleges and universities.

Jeff W. Garis
Jon C. Dalton
Editors

JEFF W. GARIS is director of the Career Center at the Florida State University in Tallahassee. He is a licensed psychologist and a holds a courtesy faculty appointment in the Department of Psychological Services in Education.

JON C. DALTON is associate professor in higher education and director of the Hardee Center for Leadership and Ethics at Florida State University in Tallahassee.

NEW DIRECTIONS FOR STUDENT SERVICES • DOI: 10.1002/ss

1

This chapter provides an overview of e-portfolio concepts and designs. It describes a model that outlines an array of dimensions for the categorization of e-portfolio systems, reviews selected systems, and makes observations regarding the importance for student affairs units to understand, collaborate, and include e-portfolio systems within their programs and services.

e-Portfolios: Concepts, Designs, and Integration Within Student Affairs

Jeff W. Garis

The evolution of Internet-based applications to higher education, classroom learning, student affairs, and career services is providing dynamic new opportunities for college student programs and services. It is common for colleges and universities to use course management software such as Blackboard in support of the entire institutional learning community, including class assignments, while providing a communications system for students, faculty, and staff. The advent of the new Web 2.0, a highly communicative system, promotes and supports student interaction through applications such as MySpace and FaceBook. Also, specialized social networking sites have been developed as career recruitment tools. For example, corporate recruiters note that social networking technology such as Linkedin provides a keyword search engine to seek job candidates throughout the world. Furthermore, most college and university career services offices employ an Internet-based system in support of student résumé databases, job listings, and recruitment programs. Examples of recruiting systems are NACElink using the Symplicity Career Services Manager system, MonsterTrak, CSO, and Experience. All of these Internet applications are rapidly changing the processes and tools that college students use in their career development and job-seeking behaviors.

In short, the practice of preparing and submitting a paper-based résumé and cover letter in support of employment is becoming outmoded. Emerging electronic portfolios hold great promise to change the national and international landscape in offering new Internet-based tools to support

NEW DIRECTIONS FOR STUDENT SERVICES, no. 119, Fall 2007   © Wiley Periodicals, Inc.
Published online in Wiley InterScience (www.interscience.wiley.com) • DOI: 10.1002/ss.245

3

college student career development. Specifically, career-related e-portfolios enable students to understand, develop, chronicle, and communicate their career attributes to others. However, career-based e-portfolios are just one of many e-portfolio applications. E-portfolios represent new and dynamic tools that support an array of higher education applications, ranging from reflective-based e-learning to assessment of learner outcomes and showcase systems supporting career development.

A comprehensive review of all e-portfolio concepts, designs, and applications is far beyond the scope of this volume. Rather, the primary focus here is on e-portfolio systems that support student affairs and university career services. However, in order to provide contextual understanding of specialized career-related e-portfolios reviewed in later chapters, the following section offers a brief discussion and overview regarding e-portfolio concepts, designs, and applications.

The Scope of e-Portfolio Systems

The scope of e-portfolios is addressed in terms of the primary goal: learning-based, assessment, or career development and employment systems.

Learning-Based Systems. Perhaps the most widespread application for e-portfolios is to support user learning. The intent of such portfolios is not to support concrete applications such as employment; rather, they are more commonly less structured in supporting user learning through reflection. For example, Cummings (2006) notes that e-portfolios provide an environment for self-reflection and often include digital representations of the visual arts, music, and storytelling. Siemens (2006) stresses the importance for supporting learning through fluid processes, and views e-portfolios as living documents emphasizing process and flow rather than the product. In these applications, e-portfolios are flexible, unstructured, and person-specific. Barrett (2006b) writes extensively regarding e-portfolios and emphasizes portfolios as vehicles that offer digital stories in support of deep learning. For Barrett, e-portfolios provide personal Web space. They are not institutionally based; rather, reflection is the heart and soul of portfolios.

It is apparent that opportunities exist for student affairs for these highly interactive Web-based applications that are becoming an integral part of college student life, and these opportunities are not necessarily linked to career services.

Assessment Applications. Assessment-oriented e-portfolios support the evaluation of student learner outcomes and may be used to support institutional assessment accreditation. Kahn (2001) addresses institutional portfolios and how they can be used in linking learning, improvement, and accountability. Kahn defines an institutional portfolio as a "focused selection of authentic work, data and analysis that demonstrates institutional accountability and serves as a vehicle for institutionwide reflection, learning and improvement" (p. 136). Yancey (2001) describes digitized student port-folios and their use in supporting and documenting interactive learning. Hult (2001) describes the use of e-portfolios in assessing student learning through writing outcomes–based program competencies and course objectives. Stu-dent portfolios are assessed by faculty and curricular assessment committees with the data used in support of departmental effectiveness, curricular design, and university accreditation. Clearly student affairs can play a prin-cipal role in supporting the university accreditation process.

Career Development and Employment Systems. E-portfolios offer a direct application in support of users' career development. Such e-portfolios are commonly used in support of the employment process in showcasing stu-dent skills and accomplishments. However, from the career development per-spective, the process of e-portfolio development may be more important than the outcome. For example, through creating an e-portfolio, student users can be introduced to the ingredients of the career development process, be instructed in core skills that support career development, and better under-stand how to plan for involvement in experiences that support skill develop-ment. Furthermore, they can be systematic and intentional in building a career portfolio that could include career goals, academic records, résumé, references, skills with supporting evidence of experience, and artifacts and work samples developed throughout the academic program. Cummings (2006) described a student-owned and managed e-portfolio that, in addition to supporting self-learning and instructor evaluation, can be used by students in support of employment. Dominick and Funk (2006) discussed an institu-tionally based e-portfolio and how students can use "folio thinking" to their advantage in developing their portfolio and in support of the employment search process. A definition of "folio thinking" would be students' ability to consider their experiences and reflect upon the resulting meaning and asso-ciated skills. Lumsden and others (2001) described a model for building an e-portfolio that supports university students' career planning and employ-ment. One of the primary components of this system is a skills matrix that enables students to learn about career-related skills and systematically build a skills matrix with supporting evidence of experiences. This system and a number of additional student affairs–based and career services–based e-portfolios are described in detail in later chapters.

Concepts and Design Considerations

Career portfolios must be placed within the context of the explosive nature of rapidly emerging e-portfolio systems that support user learning, student and institutional assessment, and career development. Indeed, the complex-ity in applications extends well beyond categories of e-portfolios intended to support learning, assessment, or showcasing career skills and accomp-lishments. But these are not mutually exclusive categories because many e-portfolio systems are used in support of all of these goals. Nevertheless,

I suggest that it is critical that the goals, intentions, and design applications of e-portfolio systems be clearly understood. E-portfolios can be considered as falling on a continuum denoting a range and extent of emphasis of e-portfolio designs. They are not offered as absolutes, forcing selection at either end of the scale. Furthermore, values are not placed on either direction, and clearly there are advantages as well as disadvantages to e-portfolio systems placed on either direction of a continuum. Figure 1.1 offers continua in considering e-portfolio designs.

Figure 1.1. Continua of e-Portfolio Design and Application

1. User Base

|──|

Student user–based   Institutionally based
What is the extent to which the user or institution is accountable for the content? Does the e-portfolio represent an "official" document?

2. Unit Base

|──|

Student affairs–based   Academic affairs or other
Which unit (student affairs, academic affairs, technical support, etc.) within the college or university holds responsibility for managing the e-portfolio system? To what extent is student affairs involved in the delivery of student e-portfolio systems? How much do units collaborate in implementing an e-portfolio?

3. System Developer

|──|

Institutionally–designed or built   Private-vendor application
Who developed and designed the e-portfolio? Is the system based on an institutional server or is the e-portfolio housed on an external vendor server?

4. Structure

|──|

Structured product–based   Unstructured, flexible,
with templates   and process oriented
To what extent does the user control the organization, design, and contents of the e-portfolio?

5. Usage

|──|

Optional use   Required usage
What is the extent to which e-portfolio use is required, ranging from institution-wide to college, department, or course-required usage? To what extent may users create an e-portfolio on their own volition?

6. Product Versions

|──|

Unlimited or multiple versions   Single product
How many versions of the e-portfolio may be created by users and/or the institution?

NEW DIRECTIONS FOR STUDENT SERVICES • DOI: 10.1002/ss

Figure 1.1. *(continued)*

7. Confidentiality and Access Control

Student controls   Institution controls
Who controls access to student e-portfolios—the user or institution? Who holds responsibility for maintaining confidentiality of student data?

8. Reflective Learning

Reflection at all levels   No reflection
To what extent does the e-portfolio encourage opportunities for reflective learning?

9. Assessment

Assessment applications included   No assessment design options
To what extent is the e-portfolio designed for and used in support of assessment of learner outcomes and/or the evaluation of institutional effectiveness?

10. Employment and Application Support

Supports showcase and employment   No user employment support
Can the e-portfolio be used in support of the user job search or application to graduate or professional school?

11. Career Development

Developmental process tool   Product rather than process oriented
To what extent is the e-portfolio designed to facilitate user career planning and support student development and career maturity?

12. Lifelong Support

Lifelong access   Temporal support
Do users have access to the e-portfolio after graduation?
To what extent can the e-portfolio be used to support lifelong learning and/or career development?

13. User Costs

No user fee   User fee–based
Are any user fees associated with access and use?

14. Institutional Cost

Free open source   License fee
Does the institution charge costs or fees for implementation of the e-portfolio? If vendor-based, are there start-up or annual licensing fees?

15. Usage Costs

Unlimited usage   Enrollment-based
Are the volume-based costs associated with the e-portfolio based on usage levels or enrollment?

(continued on next page)

Figure 1.1. (*continued*)

16. Institutional Integration

|———————————————————————————————|

Integrated into institutional database   Generic: no integration
Is the e-portfolio linked into the institution database? For example, does the e-portfolio access registrar information such as transcripts or cocurricular transcripts? Also, how much is the e-portfolio integrated into any institution-wide data management or communications software system such as Blackboard?

17. System Identity

|———————————————————————————————|

Institutional identity   User identity
Does the e-portfolio carry the institution identity such as school colors, seal, or mascot? How portable is the e-portfolio following graduation? For example, is a generic version available to users enrolling in a different institution?

18. Staff Support

|———————————————————————————————|

Centralized management   Decentralized support
Do designated staff within the institution hold responsibility for management and/or user e-portfolio support? Or are system management and user support diffused, including faculty, academic advisors, technical support staff, career services, and student affairs staff support?

Overview of Clearinghouses and Selected e-Portfolio Systems

Several selected e-portfolio systems and e-portfolio clearinghouses are noted in this chapter. A number of e-portfolio systems used primarily in support of career development are the focus of later chapters.

Clearinghouses and e-Portfolio Resources. A number of resources, centers, and clearinghouses are available for additional information regarding specific e-portfolio systems—for example:

Electronic Portfolios: Emerging Practices in Student, Faculty and Institutional Learning (Cambridge, Kahn, Tompkins, and Yancey, 2001)
E-Portfolio Clearinghouse (American Association for Higher Education, 2006)
An Overview of e-Portfolios (Lorenzo and Ittelson, 2005)
"Connectivism: Knowing Knowledge" (Siemens, 2006)
E-Portfolios—Annotated Bibliography (Penn State University, College of Earth and Mineral Sciences, 2006)
Kalamazoo College Portfolio (Kalamazoo College, 2006)
FSU Career Portfolio (Florida State University, 2006)
Inter/National Coalition for Electronic Research (2006)

In addition, Barrett (2006a) provides many online resources based on electronic portfolios.

E-Portfolio Systems Highlighted in This Volume. The e-portfolio systems highlighted in later chapters are the Florida State University (FSU) Career Portfolio, systems implemented or under development based on the FSU concept and design at the University of California San Diego (UCSD) and Georgia Institute of Technology (Georgia Tech), an e-portfolio project supported by the Connecticut Distance Learning Consortium, and an e-portfolio system created at the Pennsylvania State University.

FSU Career Portfolio. As one of the inventors of the FSU system, I am less than objective. Nevertheless, the FSU Career Portfolio represents one of the pioneering efforts and most successfully launched career portfolio systems at national and international levels. It enjoys institutionwide integration and boasts a high use. The goals of the e-portfolio are clear and directly reflect its intent to serve as a student user–based system in support of the career development process and for use as a showcase tool for employment or application to graduate study. Initial efforts in creating the FSU system date back to as early as 1997, and current use exceeds forty-five thousand student and alumni users since its 2002 launch.

UCSD Portfolio. This system was the initial adaptation of the FSU Career Portfolio model and has demonstrated similar levels of integration, use, and success at UCSD. UCSD revised the original FSU design, adding several strong features for use on its campus. Furthermore, like the FSU system, the UCSD career services office coordinates management and implementation of the system.

Georgia Tech. Georgia Tech's system, based on the FSU model, is under development. Development of this system has proved challenging in gaining institutionwide commitments for resources, agreement in system goals and design, and institutional buy-in.

Connecticut. The Connecticut Distance Learning Consortium e-Portfolio Project represents a statewide initiative with thirty one partner institutions. This project represents a broad collaborative approach and thoughtful design considerations regarding the technical platform and system goals: student learning, career planning and job search, assessment, accreditation, showcase, advising and teaching, and faculty promotion and tenure.

Penn State. Penn State's e-portfolio represents an approach different from the FSU system. The FSU system was developed as a university-wide system for all majors and provides a template that can be modified by the user. For example, the system was initiated within an academic college (Earth and Mineral Sciences) and the design is less structured. Essentially the e-portfolio offers users personal Web space without templates.

Additional Selected e-Portfolio Systems. Several e-portfolio systems are briefly discussed in order to demonstrate the range of applications developed by colleges as well as private vendors.

Kennesaw State University e-Portfolio. Dominick and Funk (2006) stress the importance of creating a user mind-set of "foliothinking" in the process of reflection and creating portfolios. Kennesaw State employs a "buffet approach" to portfolios consisting of the Online Career Portfolio (Career Services), the Pocket e-Portfolio (Presentation Technology Department), and the WebFolio (Instructional Design Department). The College Senior Portfolio process has five continual phases of development: Reflect, Assess, Collect, Connect, and Express (RACCE). Kennesaw State seniors produce two portfolio formats. The Pocket e-Portfolio allows students to record their work on digital media and maintain their own files on CD, USB, or Zip disk. The online Career Portfolio is a Web-based system maintained by the student and monitored by the university. Both systems can be cross-referenced for students to document their talents and skills in the areas of academics, employment, technology, and community service.

Chalk & Wire e-Portfolio2. Chalk & Wire's portfolio system was originally created as an assessment-oriented system that supported teacher preparation and education colleges' need for a program to support teaching accreditation standards. The system now has applicability to all disciplines, and although it continues to be assessment-oriented, E-Portfolio2 has applications to support users' academic, career development, and job seeking needs. Chalk & Wire's digital portfolio supports a wide array of tasks, including course work presentation and support, external fieldwork assessment, secure résumé and portfolio distribution, and downloadable versions of portfolios.

Blackboard's WebCT Portfolio. Many colleges and universities use vendor-based software such as Blackboard to support an institutionwide registration, instructional and course management, and communications system. Blackboard has developed an e-portfolio as an additional student service option. An advantage of systems such as the WebCT Portfolio is the natural interface between the course and instructional management system and the portfolio. As a result, it is relatively simple to download course information and projects into the portfolio system. However, users may not have lifelong access to their portfolio following graduation.

PebblePAD's e-Portfolio. PebblePAD, based in the United Kingdom, offers a flexible learning and reflection-based portfolio system. It refers to learners' publications as "stories," which "may be very formal because they are written for assessment; some stories will be written for employers or recruiters while other stories may be very personal and may relate to hobbies or interests." PebblePAD's e-portfolio is best described as an evidence-based Web publishing system. The system allows learners to create new records, Web folios, and blogs, and upload files to their e-portfolio asset stores (anything stored in the e-portfolio is named an asset).

Kalamazoo College Portfolio. Kalamazoo College is regarded as a pioneer in the development and implementation of an institutionwide portfolio system. Its portfolio was developed through a grant from the Fund for the Improvement of Post-Secondary Education (FIPSE). According to the *Kalamazoo College Portfolio* (Kalamazoo College, 2004), the innovative, Web-based, and nationally recognized "K" Portfolio starts before orientation with a "Foundations Essay" and culminates with a final "Senior Connections" response to four years at Kalamazoo. In eight required gateway points, students create their own home pages, link their best work, summarize their academic goals and plans of study, write about the choice of a major, capture their intercultural experience on paper, reflect on their career readiness, and discuss plans for their senior individualized projects. Many departments link significant course work to the portfolios of their majors.

Many student portfolios contain information and entries beyond this framework and course work at Kalamazoo College. Entries can include:

- Outstanding papers, lab reports, oral presentations, and other course work
- Photos from study abroad, internships, and other pivotal experiences
- Reflections on important relationships and experiences
- Symposia, conference, or SIP presentations
- Experiential education activities such as service-learning and an integrative cultural research project
- Application essays for leadership positions such as residence advisor or peer leader
- Self-assessment by athletes with coaches

Table 1.1 provides an example of an institutionwide systematic approach to the integration of an e-portfolio system at Kalamazoo College.

CSO's Folio21. There is an array of vendors such as CSO that have developed systems to support college and university career services offices. CSO markets software in support of the recruitment processes, including job listings, student résumé databases, employer databases, and on-campus recruiting process. It added a portfolio system to its application. CSO offers Folio21 (2006) and notes:

> E portfolios are exploding on the scene across campuses nationwide providing students with new ways to showcase their work and to differentiate themselves when seeking employment. A recent survey of nationwide university leaders indicated that 79% want to take advantage of e-portfolio's cutting edge technology to innovate their universities. Students, career centers and faculty are experiencing the far-reaching benefits and limitless possibilities of e-portfolio leader Folio21, whose web based solution enables students to: Quickly and easily create an online portfolio, effectively highlight work and experiences, easily customize views for different employers, keep their portfolio secure, track who views it and how often, access it anywhere, anytime.   •

NEW DIRECTIONS FOR STUDENT SERVICES • DOI: 10.1002/ss

Table 1.1 Kalamazoo College e-Portfolio System

Class	Portfolio Requirements and Recommendations	What It Is	Who Responds to It	When
Freshman	Foundations essay	Connects high school experiences to the K plan	Advisors	Orientation
Sophomore	Foundations for intercultural understanding	Essay questions for study abroad application	CIP Staff	Sophomore winter
Junior				
Senior	Senior connections essay	Connects various parts of "K" education, reflects on K Plan and SIP, discusses growth in dimensions* and skills**	Major department, assessment committee, portfolio office of FY advior	Spring term, senior year

*Dimensions: lifelong learning, career readiness, leadership, intercultural understanding, and social responsibility.

**Skills: information literacy, quantitative reasoning, writing, and oral communication.

Folio21 provides an online way to store and portray artifacts, work, and experiences; facilitates engagement in the learning process by providing the means to reflect on learning experiences and articulate what is gained; delivers secure and customized access for viewing; ensures total portability for unlimited use after graduation; and includes up to 25 megabytes of storage, with more available for an additional fee.

Symplicity/National Association of Colleges and Universities NACElink Alliance. NACElink represents a new paradigm in offering software systems in support of career services offices' recruitment services to students and employers. Like many other private vendor-based systems, NACElink software includes a job listing system, student résumé database, employer registration system, and on-campus recruiting support system. However, it differs from private vendors in that it is a nonprofit professional association controlled by college and employer members. In 2006, NACElink announced a new partnership with Symplicity Corporation to provide software development. The concept and design of FSU Career Portfolio, the focus of Chapter Two, was licensed to Symplicity and will be included as a module within the NACElink software system. The NACElink/Symplicity e-portfolio based on the FSU model is expected to be available during 2007.

NEW DIRECTIONS FOR STUDENT SERVICES • DOI: 10.1002/ss

International Applications

Portfolio systems are emerging internationally, with portfolio projects under way in United Kingdom, Australia, the Netherlands, France, and Finland. The European Institute for e-Learning (EIfEL) is an independent, nonprofit professional association whose mission is to support organizations, communities, and individuals in building a knowledge economy and a learning society through innovative and reflective practice, continuing professional development, and the use of knowledge, information, and learning technologies.

The Europortfolio Consortium (2006) from EIfEL notes: "The world-wide emergence of the e-portfolio is transforming our current views on learning technologies. For the first time in the relatively short history of learning technologies we see the rise of a new generation of tools dedicated to valuing and celebrating the achievements of the individual from nursery school to life long and life wide learning, a technology providing a key link for individual, organizational as well as community learning. While some counties and regions are already providing the infrastructure required to offer e-portfolio access to all citizens, other regions and countries are considering it, and others have yet to discover the possibilities."

EIfEL has organized e-portfolio conferences attracting worldwide conference papers and presentations. For example, it organized an e-portfolio conference in 2006 in cooperation with Europortfolio Consortium and the British Educational Communication and Technology Agency. Portfolio vendor sponsors were Nuventive, Winvision, and Illuminate. The conference was held in Oxford in the United Kingdom, with papers addressing policy, organizations, personal and professional development, technology, employment, and other topics.

The Role of e-Portfolios in Student Affairs

This chapters in this volume discuss the importance for e-portfolio programs to be systematically integrated within colleges and universities and for student affairs units to play a lead role, or at least become involved in, the institutionwide e-portfolio system.

The Florida State University Career Portfolio reviewed in Chapter Four is a leading example of a system that was designed, developed, and implemented as a university-wide program. The portfolio was developed and is managed through a Division of Student Affairs unit, the Career Center. The users reflect the entire university community, from freshmen through graduate and professional school students. Furthermore, virtually all academic programs use the FSU Career Portfolio, including vocationally oriented majors such as business and engineering and the liberal arts as well as the fine arts. It is particularly interesting to note the extent to which the FSU Career Portfolio has been embraced by graduate and professional school programs including M.B.A. programs and the medical school.

NEW DIRECTIONS FOR STUDENT SERVICES • DOI: 10.1002/ss

Much of the success in the FSU Career Portfolio integration and high use is a result of the support that the system receives from academic programs. For example, students initiate their use of a Career Portfolio in an introductory human development course required for all majors entering the FSU College of Human Sciences. As a result, all human sciences students are systematically exposed to the Career Portfolio and as a result create linkages with the Career Center and the Division of Student Affairs. Many other faculty also require Career Portfolio use in their courses, departments, or colleges. Through such partnerships, strong linkages are forged between academic and student affairs. Clearly, the portfolio serves as a vehicle for the Division of Student Affairs to support the learning mission of the institution.

E-portfolios hold promise to strengthen ties and cooperative programming within student affairs units. For example, they can be used to document students' leadership and service experiences acquired through a range of student affairs programs. At Georgia Tech, in addition to support through academic affairs, the CareerTech e-portfolio is featured in student affairs programs, including freshman orientation.

The reflection process in e-portfolios enables student users to understand and demonstrate the learning and skill acquisition resulting from student affairs-based out-of-class experiences, ranging from working in campus recreation positions to serving as residence hall advisers or orientation leaders. Also, through reflection, students can document learning from academic courses.

Many of the e-portfolios that are the focus in this volume would be regarded as showcase or career portfolios. However, although the final goal of these e-portfolios is to showcase accomplishments and support employment or graduate or professional school applications, an important additional advantage and goal is the learning, maturation, planning, and skill acquisition that result from the process of creating an e-portfolio. Indeed, the process of e-portfolio creation may well be more important than the outcome or e-portfolio product. The e-portfolio provides a vehicle for student users to:

- Learn about and understand the skills that are desirable for them to acquire throughout the college experience
- Become familiar with the array of experience opportunities in support of skill development
- Become proactive in planning a set of experiences and skill acquisition throughout college in support of their career plans
- Through reflection, translate a range of experience into skills and their career plans

In short, e-portfolios represent powerful tools that support college student development as well as career development.

NEW DIRECTIONS FOR STUDENT SERVICES • DOI: 10.1002/ss

This chapter also has emphasized the types and goals of e-portfolio systems. Although the primary goal of the FSU e-portfolio is to serve as a showcase or career portfolio, it has been used in support of the university accreditation process. For example, the Florida State University Quality Enhancement Plan (Wetherell and Harrison, 2004), in support of Southern Association of Colleges and Schools (SACS) accreditation, is entitled *Leaders Educated to Make a Difference* (LEAD), and the Career Portfolio program is included: "The Career Center recently launched an innovative program— the online Career Portfolio. Using this resource, students are able to showcase the skills they have developed through coursework, research involvements, internships and work experience. . . . It is an interactive tool that allows students to record, reflect upon and evaluate their experiences both in and out of class. . . . Career Portfolios will be an integral part of LEAD plans" (Wetherell and Harrison, 2004, p. 33). As a result, e-portfolios can provide an additional student affairs–based program in support of the university SACS accreditation process, as described further in Chapter Four.

Student affairs units must assume leadership in the planning, development, implementation, and integration of an e-portfolio within the institution. This leadership could involve management of an e-portfolio program housed within a student affairs unit. It also could involve the collaboration of student affairs with other units holding responsibility for e-portfolio program management such as academic affairs or technology support services. There is considerable potential for e-portfolios to bridge student affairs and academic affairs in providing opportunities for collaboration. If e-portfolio program management is not housed within student affairs, the institution must develop a plan creating linkages to ensure that student affairs programs are integrated into a university-wide plan for e-portfolio integration, staff and faculty support, and student use.

Colleges and universities should be proactive in making choices regarding system goals and designs for their institution. For example, they must consider the primary and secondary goals of e-portfolios and all of the continua presented in this chapter in support of the development, implementation, and integration of an e-portfolio system. Student affairs units must be an important part of the planning process.

References

American Association for Higher Education. *E-Portfolio Clearinghouse.* N.d. Retrieved December 16, 2006, from http://ctl.du.edu/portfolioclearinghouse/.

Barrett, H. *Electronic Portfolios and Digital Storytelling for Lifelong and Life Wide Learning.* 2006a. Retrieved December 16, 2006, from http://electronicportfolios.com/.

Barrett, H. "Voice and Interactivity in e-Portfolios: Digital Stories with Web 2.0." Paper presented at the meeting of the European Institute for e-Learning (EIfEL) on e-Portfolios. Oxford, U.K., Oct. 2006b.

Cambridge, B. L., Kahn, S., Tompkins, D. P., and Yancey, K. B. (eds.). *Electronic Portfolios: Emerging Practices in Student, Faculty and Institutional Learning.* Washington, D.C.: American Association for Higher Education.

NEW DIRECTIONS FOR STUDENT SERVICES • DOI: 10.1002/ss

CSO. *Folio21*. N.d. Retrieved December 16, 2006, from https://www.folio21.com/Default.aspx?.

Cummings, K. "Of Tansley and Technology: E-Portfolios as the Foundation of an Ecosystem." Paper presented at the meeting of the European Institute for e-Learning on e-Portfolios, Oxford, U.K., Oct. 2006.

Dominick, J., and Funk, L. "E-Portfolio Passport to Global Citizenship: Folio Thinking for College Seniors." Paper presented at the meeting of the European Institute for e-Learning on e-Portfolios, Oxford, U.K., Oct. 2006.

Florida State University. *FSU Career Portfolio*. N.d. Retrieved December 16, 2006, from http://www.career.fsu.edu/portfolio/.

Hult, C. "Using On-Line Portfolios to Assess English Majors at Utah State University." In B. L. Cambridge, S. Kahn, D. P. Tompkins, and K. B. Yancey (eds.), *Electronic Portfolios: Emerging Practices in Student, Faculty and Institutional Learning*. Washington, D.C.: American Association for Higher Education, 2001.

Kahn, S. "Linking Learning, Improvement and Accountability: An Introduction to Electronic Institutional Portfolios." In B. L. Cambridge, S. Kahn, D. P. Tompkins, and K. B. Yancey (eds.), *Electronic Portfolios: Emerging Practices in Student, Faculty and Institutional Learning*. Washington, D.C.: American Association for Higher Education, 2001.

Kalamazoo College. *The Kalamazoo College Portfolio*. 2004. Retrieved December 16, 2006, from http://www.kzoo.edu/pfolio/.

Lorenzo, G., and Ittelson, J. "An Overview of e-Portfolios." EDUCAUSE Learning Initiative, Boulder, Colo., 2005.

Lumsden, J. A., and others. "A Blueprint for Building an Online Career Portfolio." *Journal of Career Planning and Employment*, 2001, 62(1), 33–38.

Penn State University, College of Earth and Mineral Sciences. "e-Portfolios—Annotated Bibliography." N.d. Retrieved December 16, 2006, from https://www.e-education. psu.edu/portfolios/bibliography.shtml.

Siemens, G. "Connectivism: Knowing Knowledge." Paper presented at the meeting of the European Institute for e-Learning on e-Portfolios, Oxford, U.K., Oct. 2006.

Wetherell, T. K., and Harrison, D. *Leaders Educated to Make a Difference: Quality Enhancement Plan*. Tallahassee: Florida State University, Feb. 2004.

Yancey, K. B. "Digitizing Student Portfolios." In B. L. Cambridge, S. Kahn, D. P. Tompkins, and K. B. Yancey (eds.), *Electronic Portfolios: Emerging Practices in Student, Faculty and Institutional Learning*. Washington, D.C.: American Association for Higher Education, 2001.

JEFF W. GARIS is director of the Career Center at the Florida State University in Tallahassee. He is a licensed psychologist and a holds a courtesy faculty appointment in the Department of Psychological Services in Education.

2

This chapter describes how a commitment to instructional design principles has prompted the evolution of collaborative interaction between student affairs professionals and academic faculty. Central to this collaboration are the opportunities that e-portfolios have made available.

e-Portfolios: A Collaboration Between Student Affairs and Faculty

Glenn Johnson, Jack R. Rayman

Collaboration between student affairs and faculty in higher education has evolved slowly over the years. In its more recent history, however, a significant call for more involvement is readily apparent. These more recent changes are easily chronicled through the emergence of key documents that advocate deeper levels of involvement by student affairs professionals in the teaching and learning mission of educational institutions. Initially published in 1937 and then revised in 1949, *The Student Personnel Point of View* (National Association of Student Personnel Administrators, 1937, 1949) provided an early foundation. It served to establish student affairs as an entity on campus and laid out the familiar service-oriented roles for this new unit: financial aid, career services, orientation, assessment, residential life, unions and student activities, and counseling services, among others. In doing so, it helped to define what has become a lasting notion of student affairs as a student service model, a characterization that has endured and for the most part served college and university campuses well. More recently, professional associations have advocated for models that build on this foundation of service and have progressively called on student affairs professionals for a higher level of responsibility in teaching and learning.

In 1996 *The Student Learning Imperative: Implications for Student Affairs* was published by the American College Personnel Association (1996). It contended that "the key to enhancing learning and personal development is not simply for faculty to teach more and better, but also to create conditions that motivate and inspire students to devote time and energy to educationally-purposeful activities, both in and outside the classroom" (p. 1). This report

NEW DIRECTIONS FOR STUDENT SERVICES, no. 119, Fall 2007 © Wiley Periodicals, Inc.
Published online in Wiley InterScience (www.interscience.wiley.com) • DOI: 10.1002/ss.246

17

called for student affairs "to form partnerships with students, faculty, academic administrators, and others to help all students attain high levels of learning and personal development" (p. 1) and marked an initial significant shift in thinking regarding the role of student affairs, from student service to active involvement and participation in teaching and learning.

Later the American Association for Higher Education, the American College Personnel Association, and the National Association of Student Personnel Administrators jointly published *Powerful Partnerships: A Shared Responsibility for Learning* (1998). This document echoed the earlier call for involvement such that "only when everyone on campus—particularly academic affairs and student affairs staff—shares the responsibility for student learning will we be able to make significant progress in improving it" (p. 1). The report goes on to identify principles of learning as they relate to college learning, making it evident that student affairs professionals have a role to play. The report defines learning as a social and constructive process: students should be encouraged to understand how they come to understand new concepts, and connect and make sense of their own learning.

More recently calls for action have become more explicit and directive. In 2002 the Association of American Colleges and Universities published a National Panel report, *Greater Expectations,* outlining the aims of a twenty-first-century liberal education. In this report, concerns were raised about the "fragmentation of the curriculum into a collection of independently owned courses" (p. 3). Stemming from this, recommendations were made that strongly argue for student affairs involvement in educational outcomes that result in students who are empowered, informed, and responsible. The report calls for higher education to "develop more sophisticated, nuanced ways of assessing student learning" (p. 6), build a culture of evidence, and share this responsibility for learning with all stakeholders.

Most recently, the National Association of Student Personnel Administrators and the American College Personnel Association published *Learning Reconsidered: A Campus-Wide Focus on the Student Experience* (2004). This document summarizes earlier efforts and reinforces the need for shared responsibility for teaching and learning; most important, it targets specific student learning outcomes. The report argues that collaboration is essential for their achievement to be realized: "No single arena of experience is solely responsible for producing these college outcomes" (p. 23). Assuming leadership roles to further this purpose in the areas of both teaching and assessment are natural conclusions that are reached and strongly advocated for student affairs professionals.

Getting Beyond Current Perspectives and Boundaries

This handful of key documents published by national organizations in student affairs demonstrates a concerted effort to effect a shift in the thinking about teaching and learning for student affairs professionals. The principles

NEW DIRECTIONS FOR STUDENT SERVICES • DOI: 10.1002/ss

they share and the argumentation used for why this change is needed are understood. Why, then, has the action to date been limited?

In a general sense, these documents address the context and motivation for change. They focus on the reasons that this action makes sense. But few of the documents speak directly about strategies for creating opportunities for becoming collaboratively involved in teaching and learning with our academic colleagues. For many, the reality of implementing these broad changes based on reasonable perspectives of cocurricular learning outcomes seems out of reach.

In what ways can student affairs begin the process of having influence on teaching and learning on today's college campuses? Where do valued partnerships begin to form? How is collaboration fostered? How do you get to the point where jointly planned educational experiences begin to take place? Too often in the past, the experience of student affairs with initiating programs has demonstrated Sandeen's fear that ". . . if academic affairs staff and faculty view them as disconnected from the 'real' academic program, they will most likely fail to improve undergraduates' education experience" (2004, p. 31). Furthermore, in larger institutions where research and grant acquisition often take precedence, effecting real change in teaching and learning is even more challenging.

Student affairs staff need to be able to bring more to the table than insight on student learning outside the classroom. They need tools and expertise grounded in teaching and learning. If Sandeen's prediction is correct that "in the decade ahead, student affairs staff should be expected to contribute significantly to broadened student learning experiences on their campuses" (p. 31), then student affairs professionals need to be familiar with the tools and strategies that are used to mediate teaching and learning within academic programs today. We will make the case that e-portfolio development is one of those key tools.

E-Portfolio Development

A separate but related shift in thinking about teaching and learning has also been in process: the move toward student demonstration of what is learned, that is, outcomes- or competency-based education. Coupled with this, networks and Web-based technologies have also evolved, making it much easier for students to create, store, and publish evidence of their academic work online. Combined, these demonstrations of learning through the use of online information technologies have made the implementation of student-centered electronic portfolio initiatives possible. These types of developments are now occurring on an international scale. To provide support for this rapid growth, the IMS Global Learning Consortium (n.d.) recently released an initial set of application specifications that aim to support interoperability between various e-portfolio systems as an attempt to help provide some structure for these applications.

More important to student affairs, however, e-portfolios are gaining in popularity due to the need for efficiency in conducting program evaluation and accreditation reviews. Aligning themselves with the outcomes-based perspectives of learning, accreditation agencies have mandated changes in their approaches to the accreditation process such that direct evidence of student learning must be central to program evaluation. Two of the larger accreditation agencies in higher education, the Accreditation Board for Engineering and Technology (ABET) and the National Council for Accreditation of Teacher Education (NCATE), have been moving steadily in this direction. For example, ABET (2005a) requires the examination of "representative samples of student work that reveal the spectrum of educational outcome" (p. 7). And of interest to student affairs professionals is that this spectrum of learning includes the outcomes of "understanding of professional and ethical responsibility," "the broad education necessary to understand the impact of solutions in a global and societal context," and "a recognition of the need for, and an ability to engage, in life-long learning" (2005b, p. 1). These cocurricular-oriented learning outcomes have not played a formal role within traditional engineering programs of study. In 2001 the NCATE instituted a "performance-based system of accreditation" that "requires compelling evidence of candidate performance for institutions to become accredited" (p. 1). Candidate performance requires meeting criteria related to diversity, professional practice, and appropriate disposition. Again, assessment criteria here are laden with cocurricular-oriented learning outcomes.

As a result of the increased capabilities of online technologies and the need to examine student evidence of learning, students are positioned as producers rather than consumers of knowledge, and performance- or outcome-based approaches to assessment and learning have become the expected norm in higher education. At the same time that student affairs is looking for opportunities to collaborate, colleges and universities are looking for help in implementing more developmental and less prescriptive approaches to teaching, learning, and advising.

Investment in Instructional Design

The Division of Student Affairs at Penn State University began its investment in instructional design as a foundational window into teaching and learning on campus by contributing to the hiring of a half-time position of project manager for the purpose of promoting and investigating e-portfolios in May 2002. This position was also partly funded by the university's Office of Information Technology Services; of interest to note, the position was housed in the John A. Dutton e-Education Institute within the College of Earth and Mineral Sciences. By itself, this collaborative investment demonstrates a seriousness of purpose, one in which student affairs shares a common perspective and commitment to the mission of the university. More practically, however, it also provided student affairs personnel with tangible involvement related to the tools and strategies that are used to mediate teaching and learning within the context of academic programs on campus. Furthermore, this investment set in motion the use of a set of basic instructional design principles that has also helped to outline instructional strategies for involvement and collaboration: the analysis of learning needs and goals, the development of materials and activities, the evaluation of this activity, and the development of delivery systems to meet those needs. All of this led to opportunities that previously might have gone unnoticed or undervalued.

Course Management Systems. Tools such as course management systems and other information technology portals are a first level of opportunity that student affairs can begin to capitalize on. These systems provide access to scalable robust opportunities for online learning regardless of program or campus location. With these systems in mind and instructional design expertise on hand, the following questions became reasonable for the Division of Student Affairs to ask: How might these tools be used by student affairs to package and efficiently deliver many of the programs that it has to offer? To what degree do these programs require face-to-face interaction? Are opportunities to supplement what had previously been offered only locally now possible? How does student affairs get involved?

Program Evaluation and Accreditation Processes. A second level of opportunity became evident when student affairs engaged in conversations concerning program evaluation and the new requirements related to the accreditation process for the university. Cocurricular-oriented learning outcomes surfaced not only at the university level; further involvement found similar cocurricular-oriented outcomes associated with many academic program requirements, some of these influenced by shifts in new accreditation require ments. All of this engagement led to revealing opportunities for student affairs to become involved as academic programs were looking for ways to find meaningful cocurricular experiences related to these outcomes that they could efficiently incorporate into their programs of study. Student affairs can bring much to the table, but what role will it play? And how will this role be played out?

E-Portfolios. Far and away one of the most promising opportunities for collaboration between academic programs and student affairs is the electronic portfolio. One in three undergraduate students at Penn State's largest campus are already involved in publishing academic information in their online Web space. A much smaller percentage have also already published information related to their cocurricular experiences (Johnson, 2005). Might student affairs provide better support for these students? What would this support involve? Could student affairs showcase these e-portfolios for other students to see? How many more students might publish information about involvement outside the classroom? How might this support serve to more intentionally promote higher expectations regarding cocurricular learning across the university?

As the Division of Student Affairs became involved in these various opportunities, it became imperative that a consistent and coherent voice that promoted cocurricular learning come from student affairs. As a result, the Division of Student Affairs hired a second, full-time instructional designer and began work on the development of a common set of cocurricular learning outcomes (see the appendix to this chapter). At the same time that current program opportunities began to be accounted for, many began a reevaluation process, and all programming began to be mapped to this common set of learning outcomes.

Already the initial investment in instructional design is beginning to pay dividends not only in terms of motivating internal realignment but also in the development of strategies for securing external opportunities for collaboration related to e-portfolios university-wide. Student affairs professionals have become active members in a number of university-wide committees related to e-portfolio planning, e-portfolio requirements development, and the Coordinating Committee on University Assessment. The Division of Student Affairs was also recently selected as a cohort member of the National Coalition for Electronic Portfolio Research. The work of these committees, when completed, will serve to provide further evidence that will demonstrate student affairs' seriousness of purpose, a purpose that clearly aligns itself with academic programs and shares a common commitment to the mission of the university. More significant dividends are hoped for, however, as a result of the promotion, activity, and support given e-portfolio implementation within academic program contexts. Here collaboration brings a fresh awareness and recognition of the importance of student engagement and cocurricular learning directly within the teaching and learning environment of the university.

Developing an Academic e-Portfolio Culture

The development of an e-portfolio system in cooperation with an academic unit is addressed in this section.

Readiness Within the College of Earth and Mineral Sciences. The College of Earth and Mineral Sciences (EMS) has a record of fostering a student-centered environment for teaching and learning. This goal has become an integral part of the mission of the college, and since its inception, its John A. Dutton e-Education Institute has taken a lead role in supporting faculty in creating this type of environment. This prominence also makes this instructional design unit an ideal location to house an instructional designer funded in part by the Division of Student Affairs. Administration and faculty support for student-centered approaches within the college are obvious. For example, Robert Crane, associate dean for undergraduate education, commented, "There should be more to a degree program than just a series of courses completed. We have to find ways to help students find the deeper meaning that is embedded throughout the range of possible experiences in the college" (R. Crane, personal communication, April 10, 2006). Semih Eser, associate professor of energy and geoenvironmental engineering, is featured on the college's Web site as he documents the reconsideration of his teaching style in a video montage entitled, "From Bubble Sheets to Online Portfolios" (Penn State University, College of Earth and Mineral Sciences, 2006), switching his course teaching style to an active-learning, project-oriented approach. In addition, undergraduate students in the College of Earth and Mineral Sciences have been active in using their Web space to publish what they have learned as part of their Penn State experience. According to the Web use surveys conducted by the John A. Dutton e-Education Institute since 2001, consistently over half of the EMS undergraduates have activated their Web accounts and have used this Web space to publish academic-related work (Johnson, 2005).

First Year Seminar Experience. Similar to many other college programs throughout the United States, EMS requires that all incoming students enroll in a first-year seminar for the purposes of connecting with college-level learning in a small class, interacting with a senior faculty member in the college, and being introduced to the range of university-wide services and opportunities that are available. Recently e-portfolios have become part of this experience. At a minimal level of involvement, each student posts a simple introductory Web page with a link to a résumé. In doing so, each student has been introduced not only to the concept of an e-portfolio (thinking about their education in terms of the evidence they are collecting instead of concentrating purely on doing what it takes to receive a passing grade) but also to the information technology infrastructure, a support mechanism they will come to heavily rely on.

Building a Professional e-Portfolio. The First Year Seminar involvement in e-portfolios led to the creation of a new course designed to follow up on this basic experience: EMSC 300, Building a Professional e-Portfolio. This is a one-credit course that can be taken more than once by students in the college. The course requires the inclusion of a broad range of academic and cocurricular evidence and reflective narrative that targets career goals, and it focuses attention on Penn State Career Services' "Seven Career and Essential Life Skills" (Penn State University Career Services, 2006) in the publication of an e-portfolio. Feedback becomes an essential part of the e-portfolio development process, beginning with peers evaluating each other's e-portfolios and next incorporating faculty and adviser feedback; finally connections are made with alumni mentors for a real-world evaluation and feedback of the student's e-portfolio. This final step has proven to be enlightening as well as motivating, as this places students in a position where they are using their e-portfolio to begin to network within their chosen professional community. Clearly the type of thinking the e-portfolio tool engenders—thinking about their education in terms of the evidence they can share instead of concentrating purely on doing what it takes to receive a passing grade—is required in this preprofessional context.

Evidence Guidelines for Undergraduate e-Portfolios. As more meteorology students enrolled in this course, became more involved in using e-portfolios, and involved more faculty in this process, the question of how to support these students became the next logical challenge. How does a student come to know what should be included in an e-portfolio? What evidence is important? What is it that really matters? An instructional design response to this challenge generates an intriguing question for the faculty in this program: What would faculty see in an exemplary e-portfolio in this program? What would an exemplary student link to? After one year, what would the faculty see? After two years? On completion of the program? Developing evidence guidelines forces faculty to focus not on courses completed but instead on learning outcomes that target evidence and experience. This is a fresh perspective for many faculty to take with regard to their teaching and to ensure that these opportunities exist within a program (Penn State University, Department of Meteorology, 2006).

This instructional design approach fosters a fresh examination of teaching and learning. In a sense, the e-portfolio is being used as a means to prompt faculty to articulate exit outcomes for their program. The accreditation process has changed such that the focus is now on evidence of student learning. Here, this process of identifying evidence and experiences is the same and inspires discussion that accreditation authorities would like to see take place in programs, especially those that rigidly focus on course offerings. What results is a conversation that involves preparing the whole student: a student who can learn, think critically, make decisions, and solve problems in a real-world context. This inextricably brings with it the discussion of a range of attributes, such as professionalism, ethics, interpersonal skills, and self-sufficiency. Now that there is an e-portfolio culture, there is a legitimate place for these cocurricular learning outcomes to come into the conversation within this academic program. Previously it was often difficult to identify where opportunities existed within course offerings that targeted this type of engagement. In many cases, perhaps we assumed that students would gather these attributes on their own.

Students benefit from this process as well. Rather than reinforcing the "maze savviness" in students (that is, their ability to find the easy way through the mass of requirements), this process now puts students in a position that requires them to provide evidenced-based argumentation that they can use to differentiate themselves from someone who has simply taken the courses versus someone who, in the case of meteorology, can forecast the weather. Students are challenged to articulate this differentiation in terms of what they know, what they can do, and what they value as important instead of just referencing their grade point average.

Readiness Within the College of Arts and Architecture. Student teaching programs work to develop university students through a range of classroom and real-world experiences into novice teachers who are reflective practitioners. These students must learn to interact, think on their feet, and make instructional decisions based on a foundation of understandings and experience that they have been involved in as part of their program of study. The challenge for teacher educators is to assist their student teachers to make connections across their program of study.

Art and music students are familiar with the portfolio concept. Individual courses involve students in performance-related activities, either individually, with peers, or with children in schools. To support reflective thinking, the use of journaling to evaluate these experiences is often employed. Therefore, folding journaling activities into a portfolio context that contains performance-related evidence is not a large step to take. The electronic aspect of the portfolio may seem to be a larger step for these non-technical programs, but with support, the technology lends efficiencies for the manipulation and sharing of these materials.

First Year Seminar Experience. The First Year Seminar experience becomes a key entry point for the introduction of e-portfolio thinking and the technologies that make it happen. All students in the College of Arts and Architecture are involved in creating electronic portfolios during this first-year experience. In music education, students create a simple Web site that chronicles "Life as a College Student" and "Life as a Music Major." Students within this music education community share their involvement with each other through e-portfolios and recognize opportunities that otherwise they might not have become involved in. Besides teaching the basic technology skills, this activity has become a low-stakes and fun way to introduce themselves to each other as well as become more aware of opportunities in the music education community and the university as a whole.

Building Professional e-Portfolios. Rather than develop a new course to support the putting together of a professional e-portfolio, the music education program, as part of the process of remapping their curriculum, decided to include the e-portfolio as a central piece of the program. This program has positioned the e-portfolio such that it "can serve as an organizer, a goal setter, and a descriptor. It helps them collect evidence of their teaching skills, musicianship, technology skills, relationships with students in the schools in which they practice teach, assessment abilities, professional development, and curriculum planning" (Penn State University, Music Education Program, 2006). As a result, goals were established for each year of the program so that students could develop, build on, and demonstrate attainment of these goals from what they had learned in the courses they took, as well as what they had learned from their experiences outside the classroom. Most important, this process focused not on courses but instead on experience, evidence, and reflection. What resulted is a framework that students can use to help make the connections across what they have learned in their courses as well as with what they have experienced in the real world. The e-portfolio now provides program faculty with a window to review and provide feedback on a student's complete developmental process: "The e-portfolio provides a structure for preservice teachers to reflect regularly on their strengths and weakness as they select evidence for their portfolio. It enables them to authentically assess their own progress" (Penn State University, Music Education Program, 2006).

Evidence Guidelines for Undergraduate e-Portfolios. The music education program lists four goals for the e-portfolios of final-year students:

- To provide students with an opportunity to collect, select and reflect upon what they have learned at Penn State.
- To provide students with an opportunity to display evidence of their teaching skills in various musical settings.
- To provide students with a means of marketing themselves as music educators with prospective employers.
- To provide students with a strategy of continuing their own reflective professional development after graduation [Penn State University, Music Education Program, 2006].

Employing a different strategy, the art education program provides students with a teaching-learning portfolio tapestry framework (Penn State University, Art Education Program, 2006). This framework is a matrix that students use to collect and connect evidence of their learning throughout their program of study. This matrix is bordered on the horizontal axis above by the five elements of the Penn State Teacher Preparation Model:

- Educators are lifelong learners.
- Educators understand how students develop and learn.
- Educators possess discipline knowledge and pedagogical understanding.
- Educators manage and monitor learning and development.
- Educators are members of learning communities.

And this is juxtaposed on the vertical axis of the matrix with the conceptual threads that run through the art education program—areas such as instructional methods, technology, and assessment but also diversity, identity, and collaboration (Penn State University, Art Education Program, 2006).

The exit outcomes from both of these programs represent a culmination of the learning that takes place throughout each program of study. (It would be unrealistic to assume that students would be able to achieve all of these in a single capstone experience, although in the past, this has sometimes been the case.) Furthermore, the outcomes also represent a healthy dose of engagement and involvement outside the classroom throughout the college experience, an attention to career planning and professional development after college, and the development of skills over time that will support the persistence of each of these attributes—all items of great interest to student affairs. A student's e-portfolio becomes the representation of this effort—the evolution of his or her professional identity.

Creating Opportunities for Collaboration

Student-centered programs assist graduate students who have developed strategies for learning beyond their college preparation. In order to do this, they not only must make connections between what they have learned in the courses they take but also make connections between what they have experienced at university and what takes place in the real world. From a program-level perspective, e-portfolios can be strategically used as a mechanism to support the development of these types of learners: preprofessionals who have developed a sense of strategic awareness and have adopted a nature that is critically curious. Isn't this what characterizes lifelong learners?

As discussion of and activity related to e-portfolios continue to evolve, opportunities for collaboration avail themselves because academic programs require effective methods for supporting the integration of the understandings, skills, and attributes that are gained as a result of student engagement and involvement both inside and outside the classroom. As discussion and activity related to satisfying accreditation and program evaluation needs begin to evolve, this too leads to opportunities for collaboration where student affairs experience and expertise can influence curricular decision making and programming. As a result of the development of an e-portfolio culture in these programs, there are now rich opportunities to become involved in a conversation where cocurricular learning outcomes are an inextricable and explicit part of the academic program. Having helped to develop, support, and legitimize this culture, student affairs may become a legitimate partner in these discussions. E-portfolios and instructional design have helped to make this seat at the table more viable.

Future plans include a collaboration with academic programs to lead an investigation examining the administrative efficiencies that might be obtained if e-portfolios were more directly connected to the accreditation requirements of Accreditation Board for Engineering and Technology and National Council for Accreditation of Teacher Education programs. In addition, student affairs is taking a leadership role in evaluating the impact that e-portfolio systems have on the level of awareness, expectation, and engagement in cocurricular learning outcomes in general.

The process of change is slow, but evidence of the profit from initial investments is slowly being seen. E-portfolios are now referenced in the strategic plan of the university. Many more programs encourage student involvement in the development of e-portfolios, and numerous programs now require it. New audiences beyond that of undergraduate populations are also becoming involved. The use of e-portfolios by graduate students is being encouraged and supported. In addition, e-portfolios have become an instrumental learning tool for several professional certificate distance education programs, and through collaboration, their use seems destined to become pervasive throughout higher education.

Appendix: Cocurricular Learning Outcomes, Division of Student Affairs, Pennsylvania State University

Knowledge Acquisition/Application
Students will:
- Develop an understanding of knowledge from a range of disciplines/areas
- Demonstrate the ability to integrate and apply ideas and themes across the curriculum and cocurriculum

Cognitive Competency
Students will:
- Acquire learning skills to assist in their academic success
- Develop critical and reflective thinking abilities
- Apply effective reasoning skills

Life Skills and Self-Knowledge
Students will:
- Determine their career interests
- Acquire career management skills
- Develop the ability to manage and resolve interpersonal conflicts
- Cultivate a propensity for lifelong learning
- Develop personal health, fitness, wellness and leisure habits and identify health risks
- Improve self-understanding and awareness by developing an integrated personal identity (including sex, gender, sexual orientation, race, ethnicity, culture and spiritual)
- Exhibit responsible decision-making and personal accountability

Personal Integrity and Values
Students will:
- Acquire ethical reasoning skills
- Improve their ability to manage their emotions effectively
- Develop a sense of personal integrity and clarify their personal values
- Appreciate creative expression and aesthetics
- Demonstrate compassion and empathy for others

Intercultural Development
Students will:
- Possess multicultural awareness and knowledge
- Develop sensitivity to and appreciation of human differences
- Exhibit the ability to work effectively with those different from themselves
- Demonstrate a commitment to social justice

Leadership and Active Citizenship
Students will:
- Communicate effectively with others both verbally and in writing
- Demonstrate an understanding of group dynamics and effective teamwork
- Understand leadership theory and styles

NEW DIRECTIONS FOR STUDENT SERVICES • DOI: 10.1002/ss

- Identify their own leadership style when working with others
- Develop a range of leadership skills and abilities such as effectively leading change, resolving conflict, and motivating others
- Assume a sense of civic responsibility and a commitment to public life

References

Accreditation Board for Engineering and Technology. *Accreditation Policy and Procedure Manual: 2006–2007 Manual.* 2005a. Retrieved June 5, 2006, from http://www.abet.org/forms.shtml.

Accreditation Board for Engineering and Technology. *Applied Science Accreditation Criteria: 2006–2007 Criteria.* 2005b. Retrieved June 5, 2006, from http://www.abet.org/forms.shtml.

American Association for Higher Education, American College Personnel Association, and National Association of Student Personnel Administrators. *Powerful Partnerships. A Shared Responsibility for Learning.* Washington, D.C.: American Association of Higher Education, American College Personnel Association, and National Association of Student Personnel Administrators, 1998. Retrieved December 22, 2006, from http://www.myacpa.org/pub/documents/taskforce.pdf.

American College Personnel Association. *The Student Learning Imperative: Implications for Student Affairs.* 1996. Retrieved December 22, 2006, from http://www.acpa.nche.edu/sli/sli.htm.

IMS Global Learning Consortium. *IMS e-Portfolio Specification.* N.d. Retrieved June 5, 2006, from http://www.imsglobal.org/ep/index.html

Johnson, G. "Twelfth Survey of Undergraduate Student Use of Penn State Web Space Accounts. December 2005." e-Education Institute, Pennsylvania State University, June 2006. Retrieved December 22, 2006, from https://www.e-education.psu.edu/portfolio/usagesurvey_june06.html.

National Association of Student Personnel Administrators. *The Student Personnel Point of View.* 1937. Retrieved December 22, 2006, from http://www.naspa.org/pubs/StudAff_1937.pdf.

National Association of Student Personnel Administrators. *The Student Personnel Point of View.* 1949. Retrieved December 22, 2006, from http://www.naspa.org/pubs/StudAff_1949.pdf.

National Association of Student Personnel Administrators and the American College Personnel Association. *Learning Reconsidered: A Campus-Wide Focus on the Student Experience.* 2004. Retrieved December 22, 2006, from http://www.naspa.org/membership/leader_ex_pdf/lr_long.pdf.

National Panel. *Greater Expectations: A New Vision for Learning as a Nation Goes to College.* Washington, D.C.: Association of American Colleges and Universities, 2002. Retrieved December 22, 2006, from http://www.greaterexpectations.org/.

National Council for Accreditation of Teacher Education. *NCATE at 50.* 2001. Retrieved June 5, 2006, from http://www.ncate.org/documents/15YearsofGrowth.pdf.

Penn State University, Art Education Program, College of Arts and Architecture. *Teaching/Learning Portfolio Tapestry Frame with Examples.* Retrieved December 22, 2006, from http://www.sova.psu.edu/arted/undergrad/nodes.htm.

Penn State University, Career Services. "Seven Career and Essential Life Skills." Retrieved December 22, 2006, from http://portfolio.psu.edu/build/psuresources/create1.html.

Penn State University, College of Earth and Mineral Sciences. *From Bubble Sheets to Online Portfolios.* Retrieved December 22, 2006, from http://www.ems.psu.edu/features/eser/.

Penn State University, Department of Meteorology, College of Earth and Mineral Sciences. *Meteorology e-Portfolios—Evidence Guidelines.* Retrieved December 22, 2006, from http://www.met.psu.edu/dept/undprog/meteo_eportfolios.html.

Penn State University, Music Education Program, College of Arts and Architecture. *e-Portfolio—Partnership for Music Teacher Excellence.* Retrieved December 22, 2006, from http://www.music.psu.edu/musiced/e-portfolio.html.

Sandeen, A. "Educating the Whole Student: The Growing Academic Importance of Student Affairs." *Change,* 2004, *36*(3), 28–33.

GLENN JOHNSON *is project manager of Penn State's e-Portfolio Initiative.*

JACK R. RAYMAN *is director of career development and placement services and affiliate professor of counseling psychology and education at Pennsylvania State University, University Park.*

3

The Connecticut Distance Learning Consortium and thirty-one institutional partners are using e-portfolios for a wide variety of learning and assessment purposes.

Enhancing Learning and Assessment Through e-Portfolios: A Collaborative Effort in Connecticut

Diane J. Goldsmith

The most positive result of the e-portfolio project for students was their ability to make a connection between their coursework and the program goals and institutional outcomes. Often students only think they are completing course requirements and they are totally unaware of the bigger picture of program and institutional outcomes that are being achieved.

Survey of e-portfolio users, Tunxis Community College, 2006

E-portfolios are a rich, flexible tool for teaching, learning, and assessment. They provide institutions with a way to assess how well they are educating their students. At the same time, they provide students with a way to better understand their educational experience and achievements and how these are linked to their personal goals. With e-portfolios, students have access to a virtual platform for sharing their goals, achievements, and insights with advisers and counselors to ensure that they are meeting their career and educational goals. And this same tool allows students to demonstrate their achievements to others, including future employers. Implementing e-portfolios requires planning, new procedures, new ways of thinking, additional resources, and training both faculty and students. Institutions working in collaboration can bring an added richness to the process. The ability to share resources, implementation processes, insights into training, and tips for working with faculty

NEW DIRECTIONS FOR STUDENT SERVICES, no. 119, Fall 2007 © Wiley Periodicals, Inc.
Published online in Wiley InterScience (www.interscience.wiley.com) • DOI: 10.1002/ss.247

31

and students has made a major difference to the Connecticut institutions involved in a collaborative e-portfolio project.

At Tunxis Community College, all students enrolled in the computer information systems program are using e-portfolios to develop a collection of work as both a showcase for potential employers and a programmatic assessment tool. The dental hygiene students are using e-portfolios throughout their program to demonstrate their competencies. Albertus Magnus College is exploring the potential of using e-portfolios to assess student learning outcomes in the general education program. At Capital Community College, e-portfolios are being used to improve student learning in the College Success course, a first-year orientation experience. At Northwestern Connecticut Community College, e-portfolios are being used as a learning connection between courses that form a student's learning community. E-portfolios are being used by the nursing program at Three Rivers Community College to improve learning and for programmatic assessment and by the nursing program at Fairfield University for assessment and career purposes.

Why are e-portfolios an important learning and assessment tool for institutions both now and for the future? Higher education institutions in Connecticut began the process of responding to these questions in 2002 with the help of a grant from the Fund for Improvement of Post Secondary Education (FIPSE). Under the auspices of the Connecticut Distance Learning Consortium (CTDLC), eleven public, private, baccalaureate, and associate-degree-granting institutions began a collaborative project to answer these questions in terms of supporting students, improving teaching and learning, and promoting assessment. As the e-portfolio requirements of the partner institutions began to be clarified, the CTDLC created an e-portfolio platform to meet these needs and a network of e-portfolio project directors to support their implementation efforts. This chapter examines how the responses to these two questions have evolved and expanded over the past four years and how the CTDLC has supported institutional efforts to implement e-portfolios for learning and assessment purposes. Since the inception of the project, participating partners have expanded from eleven to thirty-one.

Assessment

Assessment in higher education is often used to mean two separate activities. First, the assessment of the individual student asks, How well is this student learning what we are (or at least think we are) teaching? Although helping the student understand what steps to take to improve is not always part of assessment, it is a critical element of individual assessment. Faculty have been responsible for this type of assessment for centuries using tests, essays, research papers, projects, experiments, problem sets, case studies, and other evaluative activities that result in a score or grade. But many would argue that faculty place too much reliance on methods such as tests, which require students to respond to questions about what they know rather than more authentic types of assessment that evaluate students on how well they perform messy, real-world, intellectually challenging tasks (Wiggins, 1990). For example, instead of a test with questions on a historical period, authentic assessment methods might ask a student to use that knowledge to analyze an original document from that period. This requires students to use their knowledge and skills to construct meaning and produce a work that has value beyond a grade or score (Newmann and Wehlage, 1993). In effect, they are asked to do what historians do: create knowledge. Authentic assessment therefore results in a product and, if evaluated against specific criteria such as can be delineated in a rubric, a path for improvement. Authentic assessment is also often individualized to take into account the goals of individual students.

Second, *assessment* is used to refer to the set of activities that an institution, department, or program uses to evaluate itself. It asks two questions: How well is this program, department, or institution teaching what we say we want our students to learn? And, How can we use these data to improve our program and our teaching? While some institutions, such as Alverno College (2006), have done this type of assessment since the 1970s, many others have not. And at least in the view of some, these efforts have been inadequate: "Despite increased attention to student learning results by colleges and universities and accreditation agencies, parents and students have no solid evidence, comparable across institutions, of how much students learn in colleges or whether they learn more at one college than another" (Miller, 2006, p. 15).

Implicit in a desire for institutional assessment that allows for evidence that is comparable across institutions is a method such as standardized testing that generates scores, so we can learn that on the average, students at college A score X in critical thinking versus those at university B who score Y. However, like the proponents of authentic assessment, opponents of such methods argue that institutional assessment too must take into account the individualized missions of higher educational institutions and the specific learning objectives of programs and departments. This second view is exemplified by the *Nine Principles of Good Practice for Assessing Student Learning* (Astin and others, 1996), developed by the American Association of Higher Education. These principles place an emphasis on aligning assessment with the values and mission of the institution. They emphasize that assessment must be multidimensional, integrated, and authentic; it is best when it takes place throughout a student's educational experience rather than a one-shot summative evaluation; and it involves a collaboration of faculty and staff throughout the institution.

Portfolios and Assessment

All portfolios, paper based or electronic, generally share three basic characteristics that allow them to be used as an assessment tool: (1) the ability to collect materials created for a variety of reasons over time, (2) the ability to select from this collection and organize it, and (3) the ability to surround the work itself with additional information and content, including introductions and reflection. Portfolios are more than just giant files. Creating a portfolio requires that students select from the work they have saved in a portfolio and organize the materials for a specific purpose. This can include exhibiting the range of their skills and achievements, creating a representation of their best work, or demonstrating growth or change over time. Through prompts for reflections and introductions, faculty can encourage students to reengage with their work in a meaningful way. These prompts can ask students to examine a single piece of work in their portfolio or the entire collection and describe their learning process; discuss how they would approach similar assignments differently; highlight or criticize specific elements of their work; explain how this work meets a specific requirement, objective, or assignment; situate their work at a specific time in their development; or help the reader understand this particular portfolio. It is this continual meaningful reengagement, as students create and recreate their portfolios, that both enhances the learning process and allows portfolios to be used for authentic assessment.

A Model for Individual and Programmatic Assessment

Portfolios, as an assessment tool, have the advantage of being able to be used simultaneously for both individual and programmatic assessment. As the model in Figure 3.1 indicates, this has advantages for both the individual and the program. As specified in the American Association for Higher Education (Astin and others, 1996) criteria for assessment, the model first requires that the program to be assessed clearly define its objectives. Next, it requires defining the competencies that students need to demonstrate in order to meet these objectives. Then it requires the program to specify the types of artifacts, that is, authentic examples of work, that students need to provide to demonstrate their learning. Portfolios are submitted to an instructor or committee for review and evaluation to answer the question of how well the student has demonstrated mastery of the required competencies. These same portfolios are saved and reviewed to answer the question of how well the program is doing at providing the appropriate learning opportunities for the specified competencies. Finally, portfolios provide a showcase for students and for the program or institution.

The "e" Advantage

Although this process is possible with paper-based portfolios, the electronic feature provides major advantages. For the institution, it eliminates closets full of looseleaf binders or file folders and moves storage to disks, hard drives, servers, and storage area networks. It allows the portfolio owner to

Figure 3.1. Portfolio.Org as a Tool for Program Assessment

> **Program objectives**
> What should we teach in this program?
> What should students learn?

> **Individual assessment**
> Is student A learning what we
> say we want him or her to learn?

> **Programmatic assessment**
> Is our program teaching what
> we say we want to teach?

> **How do we know?**
> Program Competencies
> What characteristics, skills, knowledge,
> attitudes, or values will the student
> demonstrate so you know he or she
> has achieved the outcomes?

> **e-Portfolio**
> Students compile a portfolio of artifacts demonstrating their
> competencies in the areas defined by the program outcomes. This
> process allows reflection and self-evaluation.

> **How well has student A achieved
> or demonstratred these
> competencies?**
> • Portfolio reviewed or graded
>   using rubrics or some other
>   method allowing for inter-rater
>   reliability among faculty
> • Comments on individual
>   strengths and weaknesses
> • Plan for individual improvement

> **How well is this program doing at
> introducing and providing adequate
> learning experiences for students to
> master these competencies?**
> • Aggregate scores on competencies
>   or randomly select and score
>   anonymously
> • Use raw data plus SIS data to
>   analyze specific issues
> • What are the program's strengths
>   and weaknesses?
> • Plan for programmatic improvement

> **Students use their portfolios to
> tell their story to employers or
> graduate schools**
> Experience of creating it; also
> practice in discussing their
> achievements, skills, and talents.

> **Programs use results for e-portfolio
> assessment to showcase their
> students' achievements**
> With permission, program can showcase
> a variety of student responses; results
> can be used for accreditation.

Source: Goldsmith (2006, p. 5).

keep work over time without keeping track of individual pieces of paper or files on an individual computer. Any type of digital material or material that can be digitized can be placed in an e-portfolio, a major advantage in a world where many students are creating digital objects. The "e" makes

portfolios available any time and anywhere for both the owners of the portfolios and for those viewing and reviewing them. Their electronic nature
also allow portfolios to be genuine, easily available showcases for purposes
outside the institution, such as job searches. Rather than carting folios or
binders about, students can invite guests to click on a link and review their
work online at their leisure. The move to an electronic format has also
meant that the notion of what a portfolio is has expanded and continues to
change. E-portfolios can be an extremely flexible tool, with a student's single e-portfolio used for a multitude of purposes for a variety of audiences.
Our partner institutions' students are not only using e-portfolios in their
classes, but also working with career counselors, as part of their advising
process, for cocurricular activities, athletics, special projects, and semesters
abroad, all facilitated by the move to Web-based e-portfolios.

Connecticut's Experiences

An instructor who responded to a survey of e-portfolio users in spring 2006
had this to say: "The e-portfolio gave the students a chance to exercise
reflective learning. The students were able to see their growth in different
areas over time. As an instructor, I found the guest invitations an invaluable
tool in gaining insight to assignments and topics being covered in class. The
reflective piece also helped reveal characteristics of the student that may
have not been revealed in class."

The participating institutions have found several major advantages of
using e-portfolios for assessment purposes. Portfolios allow assessment
of the students' actual work, achievements, or products. They can be used
simultaneously to assess individual achievement (that is, how well the student is doing in meeting course or programmatic objectives) and to determine how effective courses, programs, departments, or institutions are in
providing learning opportunities to ensure that students meet their goals
and objectives. They require that the students understand the goals and
objectives for which they are creating a portfolio. For example, some
assessment methods may test a specific skill or scope of knowledge such
as critical thinking skills, and they may require a faculty member to collect
work that she believes evidences these skills or knowledge. E-portfolios
require that students understand these skills or knowledge, can select work
that demonstrates their skills or achievements in this area, and can reflect
on why they have chosen this particular piece of work to meet the stated
objective. As one of our community colleges found, this means that faculty
need to discuss programmatic and general education objectives with their
students to ensure they are clear about what is required to meet these
objectives and how they will be assessed. They also need to ensure the students see how an individual course fits into this larger picture.

E-portfolios can be individually graded and commented on to provide
students with feedback as to their competencies. Collectively e-portfolios

can be reviewed, using holistic scoring methods, rubrics, or random selection, to provide the program being assessed with information as to its strengths and weaknesses. Programs can assess which objectives students are meeting well and which require programmatic improvement. For example, with the adoption of e-portfolio, the dental hygiene faculty at a partner community college proposed a total curriculum revision that incorporated a capstone project course in the final semester prior to graduation. This course will focus on the students' best work, demonstrating their achievement of program goals and institutional outcomes for view on e-portfolio.

E-portfolios also allow revision over time. Instead of an assignment being handed in, graded, and then filed away, it can be added to a portfolio and revised, revisited, and reflected on. A writing faculty at one of the participating institutions has students complete a writing assignment and submit it for grading and comments. When it is returned, the students must add it to their e-portfolios and respond to a series of questions to help them reflect on their writing and how to improve it. At the end of the semester, these students must reflect on their entire semester's work. This is a highly metacognitive process that requires students to engage meaningfully with each piece of their work three times.

For students, compiling a portfolio provides the opportunity to connect their work in individual courses to the institutional outcomes. Students describe their ability to understand these connections as well as the connections between their own lives and their academic work. When students at one of the community colleges during their first semester of using e-portfolios were asked in a survey in spring 2006 what they liked best about them, they commented on how e-portfolios "made me think about myself and what I was doing," allowed the student to ". . . store work related to a specific goal," helped them make connections in that "I could group work and send it grouped," helped them in "organizing thoughts and goals," and "allows you to see how far you have advanced."

Ultimately the creation of e-portfolios results in both a product that an institution can use to demonstrate how well it is meeting its goals and a showcase for students to demonstrate their skills for personal or employment purposes. Even in the first semester of creating a portfolio, a student commented, "I really like using e-portfolios because it gives me a chance to show off the work that I am most proud of" (survey of e-portfolio users, spring 2006). Overall, as the participating institutions began to implement e-portfolios as a learning and assessment tool, students who initially resisted what appeared to be more work and the need to learn one more type of software were pleased that this work resulted in a tangible demonstration of their accomplishments. Faculty who may have resisted for many of the same reasons—extra, or at least different, work, and one more technological platform to master and teach with—were pleased with how students were using e-portfolios. Faculty using e-portfolios to connect learning community courses commented in the spring 2006 survey, "Students updated the e-portfolio on a continuing basis and it was interesting to see the changes that they made throughout the semester. It was obvious that students completing the assignment were proud of their work and used the reflection, information, and comment sections to map their progress and what they learned from the new topics in the software applications class. It was most interesting that the assignments did show a connection between the learning community courses."

Challenges

Working with institutions as they began to adopt e-portfolios was reminiscent of the beginnings of online education in Connecticut. That process was spearheaded by a few faculty, and in most cases it was uneven; few institutions had plans for creating online programs and services, and in many cases those who were teaching online had neither taught nor studied online. Many of the participating institutions began their e-portfolio implementation similarly. Their process was spearheaded by a few faculty or staff with no concrete plans for institutionalizing this adoption, no support system in place, and few faculty or staff who had ever created a portfolio, paper-based or electronic.

Some institutions moved from a paper-based portfolio system to an e-portfolio one. This did require learning some new technology but not major changes in pedagogy. However, most of these institutions did not have this experience. Moving to e-portfolios necessitated changes in assignments, workloads, and assessment methods. Because the major virtue of an e-portfolio is that it makes possible saving work over time, institutions had to grapple with the questions of which work, for what purpose, and for how long. For many institutions, these are ongoing questions, and in one or two that had no clear assessment strategies, no advocates for the required changes, or no skilled change agents, the move to adopt e-portfolios failed.

Implementing e-portfolios requires that faculty, staff, and students learn to use a new software package and understand the assumptions on which it was built. For faculty, understanding the e-portfolio platform affects the way they need to construct portfolio assignments and work with assessment activities. So training of faculty must have both technical and pedagogical components. E-portfolios emphasize self-assessment, reflection, and metacognitive skills. Many incoming students lack the educational sophistication those skills require, and many faculty have not taught these skills before. Pedagogical training for faculty should include discussions of the types of questions and assignments that help students gain these skills. It is also helpful for departments to create a plan so that it is clear in which courses students will be introduced to such skills and how those skills will be practiced and enhanced as students take more advanced courses.

Too often while faculty were learning the platform, they were also trying to train students. Institutions that have been most successful at implementing e-portfolios have planned how and where training of both faculty and students will occur and clearly designated which courses and programs will implement the platform. Many institutions have planned to introduce e-portfolios in first-year orientation courses, but some, especially in community colleges, have found that a significant number of students do not come with adequate computer skills and are overwhelmed by learning the course management system, the portal, and the e-portfolio. Careful planning, preenrollment computer skills remediation, and good training have helped these institutions successfully deal with these barriers. Successful institutions also provided trained staff (often peers) who are available in specific locations at designated times to help students and faculty with e-portfolio issues. This is important even though the CTDLC offers telephone and e-mail support to users. Students and faculty tend to use the CTDLC help desk for technical problems and their own support systems for a better understanding of how to work within the system. Here again, as they implemented their learning management systems, the lessons institutions learned about help desks, training, workshops, teaching and learning centers, and peer support provided a model for an institutional e-portfolio implementation plan.

The Platform Dilemma

One major challenge for most institutions is the decision of which platform to use. When the CTDLC began this project, it decided to build a portfolio platform because the only e-portfolio platforms available were those built by individual institutions to meet their specific needs. Today, in response to the growth in demand, e-portfolio platforms are widely available (EduTools, 2007). Choosing the appropriate platform has become a complex issue. It is essential to remember that e-portfolios are a tool that needs to be matched to the institutional purpose or purposes. The following questions can form a basis from which to structure the institutional platform conversation:

- What need is driving the search for an e-portfolio platform?
- Are there future needs that must be considered? Kent State built a wonderful platform for a portfolio dedicated to career counseling and job search issues, but now the institution is considering portfolios for other uses (A. Motayar, personal communication, 2005). Does it throw out what it built, try to adapt it, or use several platforms?
- Who is the e-portfolio for: students, faculty, the institution, potential employers?
- Who is going to see it?
- Will it be reviewed and graded?
- Are students mostly technically savvy, or do many (for example, returning adult students or students who have not grown up with computers) come with more limited technical skills?
- How knowledgeable are the faculty and staff in using portfolios and adopting new technologies?

NEW DIRECTIONS FOR STUDENT SERVICES • DOI: 10.1002/ss

- How will implementation grow? Is this just for one department or program, or will it be used across the institution—for general education assessment, for example?
- Who is the change agent here?
- Who will support the implementation of e-portfolios? Who might resist? What will aid in overcoming any resistance?
- What resources are available? Does the institution have enough instructional technology staff and substantial resources, or are support staff limited?
- Will the e-portfolio be integrated into a learning management or student information system? Public institutions may want to consider initiatives that use a single e-portfolio platform to link students in K–12, community colleges, and state colleges and universities.
- Is the primary focus assessment? If so, consider connections to learning objectives, rubric builders, anonymous scoring, and how long portfolios will be kept by the institution.
- Who owns the material in the e-portfolio, and who determines who can see it? Can anyone find and see a student's portfolio, or is there protection for privacy and to inhibit plagiarism?
- Does access to students' e-portfolios conform to FERPA (Family Educational Rights and Privacy Act)? Is it compliant with the Americans with Disabilities Act?

There may be other institution-specific questions that need to be considered before buying or building a platform.

Although using these questions in analyzing institutional needs is important, it is also important not to let the question of which platform to use derail the e-portfolio project. There is no way for an institution to pick or even build a perfect platform. Given all of the options for implementing portfolios, it is impossible to ensure that everyone's needs are met 100 percent of the time. Large institutions may be able to pick more than one platform or build one that can be continually adapted to changing needs, but in most cases institutions need to pick or build what they think is best and then, as Tom Lewis (2004) says, alter practices, curriculum, and processes to work with that platform.

One faculty member noted in the 2006 survey: "It is a challenge to get people to use the rich, flexible tool 'as is' (meets 90 percent of their needs) rather than looking at it and finding reasons not to use it. When folks say, 'This is a really great tool, but we cannot use it because it lacks X,' they are often simply resisting altering existing practices, curriculum, or processes. How can we get beyond this?"

There are always trade-offs in any platform, whether institutionally built or purchased. Having students create their portfolios using HTML or HTML editors favors originality and graphic skills. Using a forms- or a template-based system requires fewer computer skills for both students and faculty but may not tap on creativity. Cost is an issue, and decisions on platforms may rest not only on the costs but also on how those costs are distributed. There is the cost of developing, buying, or, in the case of open source, adapting the software. There is the cost of the hardware and the staff to run it. An ASP (application service provider) model, such as the CTDLC's, shares the costs of hardware, software development, and support, but at the cost of a unique solution for each institution.

Regardless of how an institution decides to distribute the costs of the software and hardware, there are additional costs that must be figured into adopting e-portfolios, including the need for technical support and training for faculty and students. Participating institutions that have been the most successful in implementing e-portfolio have clearly defined places and times when students can get help with e-portfolios. These are often staffed by trained students. Faculty need technical training and support, but unless they are moving from a paper-based system, there is an even greater need for pedagogical support and training to help faculty and staff understand how to use portfolios effectively.

Success Breeds Success

As faculty, staff, and students discovered the richness of the tool for teaching, learning, assessment, and as a showcase, their enthusiasm provided the major impetus to move the adoption of e-portfolios in other parts of their institution. The advantage of working in a consortium is that each institution was able to learn from these successes and challenges. Although their institutional missions are different and their reasons for adopting e-portfolios differed greatly, the process of the participating institutions' answering and then reevaluating their responses to the question, "Why are electronic portfolios an important learning and assessment tool for institutions?" provided an enormous amount of information on how to improve the functionality of the platform and increase the impact of e-portfolios within a single institution. As one of the participants explained to the external evaluator of our FIPSE grant, "The current e-portfolio is light years ahead of where we started and any one of us working alone would not have gotten half as far" (Brown, 2006).

References

Alverno College. "Ability Based Curriculum." 2006. Retrieved September 13, 2006, from http://www.alverno.edu/about_alverno/ability_curriculum.html.

Astin, A., and others. "Nine Principles of Good Practice for Assessing Student Learning." 1996. Retrieved September 7, 2006, from http://www.fctel.uncc.edu/pedagogy/assessment/9Principles.html.

Brown, J. "Third Year/Final Evaluation Report on FIPSE Funded Project: 'Supporting Online Learners: A Statewide Approach to Quality Academic Support Services.'" 2006. Unpublished report, Connecticut Distance Learning Consortium, Newington, Conn.

EduTools. "e-portfolio: EduTools e-Portfolio Review." 2007. Retrieved January 29, 2007, from http://eportfolio.edutools.info/static.jsp?pj=16&page=HOME.

Goldsmith, D. J. "Using e-Portfolio for Assessment." 2006. Retrieved January 29, 2007, from http://www.eportfolio.org/references/Usinge-portfolioforassessment.pdf.

Lewis, T. "E-Portfolios: What the Heck Are They, and If You Have Them, Why Would Anyone Use Them?" 2004. Retrieved September 13, 2006, from http://portfolio.washington.edu/goodwork/nwacc-2004-e-portfolio-presentation/104004.html.

Miller, C. "A National Dialogue: The Secretary of Education's Commission on the Future of Higher Education 9/9/06 Draft Report." 2006. Retrieved September 11, 2006, from http://www.ed.gov/about/bdscomm/list/hiedfuture/reports/0809-draft.pdf.

Newmann, F. M., and Wehlage, G. G. "Five Standards of Authentic Instruction." *Authentic Learning,* 1993, *50*(7), 8–12. Retrieved September 11, 2006, from http://pdonline.ascd.org/pd_online/diffinstr/el199304_newmann.html.

Wiggins, G. "The Case for Authentic Assessment." *Practical Assessment, Research and Evaluation,* 1990, 2(2). Retrieved September 9, 2006, from http://PAREonline.net/getvn.asp?v=2&n=2.

DIANE J. GOLDSMITH *is dean of planning, research, and assessment at the Connecticut Distance Learning Consortium. Newington, Connecticut.*

NEW DIRECTIONS FOR STUDENT SERVICES • DOI: 10.1002/ss

4

This chapter describes the development of a successful e-portfolio system, with over forty-seven thousand users within five years of implementation and how it has been integrated as a university-wide program.

Development and Implementation of an e-Portfolio as a University-wide Program

Jill A. Lumsden

The Florida State University's e-portfolio program, FSU Career Portfolio (Lumsden and others, 2001), is a student-managed portfolio system that students and alumni can use to reflect on and integrate their learning experiences and document and showcase their skills and accomplishments (Reardon, Lumsden, and Meyer, 2005). Not only has this program proven to be a powerful tool in supporting students' career planning and their transition to employment or graduate or professional school, but it has had other benefits and uses throughout the university. Through the Career Portfolio, students are introduced to important skills they need to develop and are encouraged to document the development of those skills through reflection and articulation of their experiences. Students can upload samples of their work, include a résumé or curriculum vitae (CV), display an academic transcript or service transcript, provide reference contact information, and create an introductory profile. Versions of a student's Career Portfolio can be made available to referred users, whom the student designates, such as employers, faculty members or instructors, or graduate or professional school admissions committees. Students maintain ownership of their portfolio entries and control who sees what in each of three possible versions of their Career Portfolio (Lumsden, Meyer, and Garis, forthcoming).

The FSU Career Portfolio was implemented campuswide in April 2002. Five years after implementation, over forty-seven thousand students have

NEW DIRECTIONS FOR STUDENT SERVICES, no. 119, Fall 2007 © Wiley Periodicals, Inc.
Published online in Wiley InterScience (www.interscience.wiley.com) • DOI: 10.1002/ss.248

begun these portfolios. The FSU Career Portfolio was made possible through the initiative of the university president and the support of key administrators in both student and academic affairs. Its success is due to several factors, including top-down, university-wide support; the vision and leadership of the Career Center; partnership with University Information Systems; feedback and buy-in from key stakeholders (students, staff, faculty, and employers); effective marketing and implementation activities; and targeted evaluation since implementation (Reardon, Lumsden, and Meyer, 2005).

This chapter describes one example of an e-portfolio developed and implemented at a large, graduate research university with over forty thousand students, located in the Southeast United States. Though originating out of student affairs (the Career Center), the Career Portfolio has created partnerships with academic affairs and is used in varied ways, many of them unexpected. This chapter explores the history of the Florida FSU Career Portfolio; the philosophical bases and goals of the program; implementation strategies, intended and unintended; and evaluation of both students and employers is included.

History, Philosophy, and Goals

The FSU Career Portfolio Program (CPP) was in development for almost five years before its launch in April 2002. Development of the Career Portfolio was initiated in September 1997 when the president of the university approached the Career Center regarding ideas to teach and certify the development of workforce skills in FSU graduates. Proposals by Career Center staff described an online portfolio system for developing and documenting students' skills and accomplishments. Several funding proposals were considered, and in December 1999, the university granted funding for a full-time position, a project manager, to lead the development of an e-portfolio program. The Career Center wanted to create a program with university-wide applications and thus decided to develop a portfolio system specific to FSU, leveraging existing technology, such as the student online security system, and integrating existing student databases.

For eighteen months, a task force varying in size from seven to nine members within the Career Center met weekly to discuss the goals, philosophy, and design of the Career Portfolio, and a prototype was developed to showcase this work. This prototype was shared with administrators, students, and employers to gather feedback and assist in further development. It was also used as the basis for the information systems department to build the technical infrastructure to support the system. The prototype provided clear and detailed specifications for the design and functionality of the system. This allowed information systems staff to understand and support the vision of the e-portfolio program. Information systems had a team of twelve programmers, technical managers, and project managers who contributed to the development of the system (two worked full-time on the Career Portfolio during the development phase). (The prototype can be viewed at www.career.fsu.edu/portfolio/index.html.) The portfolio task force sought feedback from administrators, staff, and employers throughout the development phase. Response was highly positive, with employers, faculty, administrators, and students reacting favorably to the design, philosophy, and usability of the system. Many design changes were made as a result of the feedback gathered through the development, improving the system's usability and design (Reardon, Lumsden, and Meyer, 2004).

One of the key steps in the developmental process was outlining clearly the philosophy, purpose, design considerations, and goals of the e-portfolio system. Four philosophical principles are basic to the CPP. First, the CPP encompasses a desire to create a system that enables students to develop and pursue a personal strategic career vision. Second, it is founded on a belief that the university should be dedicated to producing graduates needed in an emerging global economy characterized by lean production, information technology, and alternative ways of working (Reardon, Lenz, Sampson, and Peterson, 2006). Third, the CPP focuses on employers of college graduates who value evidence that students are ready to make effective contributions in the contemporary workplace. Fourth, the program is based on the idea that career planning services are a boundary-spanning function linking education and employment, providing connections joining education, work, and community organizations. In summary, the CPP was seen as having the potential to provide a developmental, comprehensive, learner-centered emphasis for educational and career planning services at the university (Reardon, Lumsden, and Meyer, 2004).

Design Considerations. Based on the results of early research, surveys, and development work, thirteen design considerations for the FSU Career Portfolio were developed by the portfolio task force:

1. Be student-centered, based on learning activities throughout the undergraduate and graduate school years.
2. Enable students to plan and pursue a strategic career vision.
3. Enable students to select and pursue learning activities within and outside of their formal curricula that would enhance the likelihood of their achieving personal and professional goals.
4. Be initiated and sustained by student involvement, with assistance from many university resources.
5. Be available to students in all majors, in both self-help and brief staff-assisted modes of intervention.
6. Use sophisticated technology available via the Internet.
7. Provide a method for selecting, acquiring, and documenting career skills.
8. Be available to students at any level, from lower-division students to final-term seniors, from graduate students to alumni.
9. Provide employers with documentation that FSU students are ready to make effective contributions in the workplace.

NEW DIRECTIONS FOR STUDENT SERVICES • DOI: 10.1002/ss

10. Promote career preparation throughout students' undergraduate or graduate educational experiences, not as something that can be accomplished with one visit to the Career Center.
11. Address the needs of students, faculty, employers, and the public, including parents.
12. Increase the economic productivity and career satisfaction of graduates, as well as public support for higher education.
13. Involve many different agencies and programs in the university, such as service learning (volunteer work that enhances the classroom experience), academic advising, student recruiting, job placement services, cooperative education, classroom instruction, student activities and organizations, liberal arts courses, and preprofessional training programs [Reardon, Lumsden, and Meyer, 2004, pp. 11–12].

Goals. After reaching a consensus on the general characteristics and scope of the proposed CPP, the task force specified four general program goals: FSU would seek to develop (1) a comprehensive system for helping students connect learning opportunities with employer needs; (2) a program for helping students integrate curricular and cocurricular experiences; (3) an innovative Internet-based system to promote student learning, career preparation, and employment; and (4) a high-visibility program to support student recruitment and retention.

With respect to student learning outcomes, it was determined that as a result of engaging in the CPP, students would be able to (1) develop strategic planning skills that prepare them for the job campaign or postgraduate study; (2) be aware of the importance of identifying and developing transferable career and life skills; (3) identify learning opportunities that foster career and life skills; and (4) know how to communicate and market career and life skills to potential employers or graduate or professional school admissions committees (Reardon, Lumsden, and Meyer, 2004).

A key element of the Career Portfolio has been the identification of skills that are valued in the workforce and many other life roles. These skills, which later became the Career Portfolio's career/life skills, are (1) communication, (2) creativity, (3) critical thinking, (4) leadership, (5) life management, (6) research/project development, (7) social responsibility, (8) teamwork, and (9) technical and scientific (Lumsden and others, 2001). This list, developed by the portfolio task force, was based on research on the skills that employers look for in prospective employees. In addition, eight of the nine skills (those listed above with the exception of research/project development) were rated by employers who recruit at FSU in terms of the importance of the skill and the frequency of its use within the employers' organizations. Employers validated these eight skills as important to their organizations and used frequently. (Detailed results can be found in Reardon, Lumsden, and Meyer, 2004.) The portfolio task force added the ninth skill area, research/project development, at the urging of the university president to reflect the importance of research at FSU.

Program Description

The home page of the CPP provides users with two selection options: (1) FSU Students and Alumni: Enter Portfolio and (2) Referred User: View Portfolios (see Figure 4.1). Each of these options is described below. (A preview of the Career Portfolio is available at http://www.career.fsu.edu/portfolio/walkthru/index.html.)

FSU Students and Alumni: Enter Portfolio. This selection requires the user to log in through the FSU secure Web portal and takes the user to the main menu (Figures 4.2 and 4.3). At the main menu, students can access the first-time-user tour through a link that says "First Time User? Take This Tour!" This selection is intended to provide an introduction and overview of the system and motivate students to become involved in the program. This ten-step "tour" also provides information about the nine career and life skills and the five experience categories through which students develop their skills: courses, jobs/internships, service/volunteer work, memberships/activities, and interests/life experiences. Also at the main menu, students have options to build, manage, or learn in relation to their career portfolio.

Figure 4.1. Career Portfolio Home Page

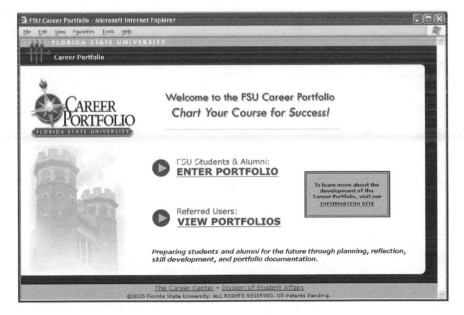

Figure 4.2. Career Portfolio Main Menu: View 1

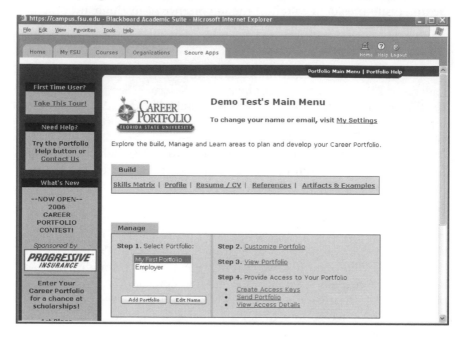

Figure 4.3. Career Portfolio Main Menu: View 2

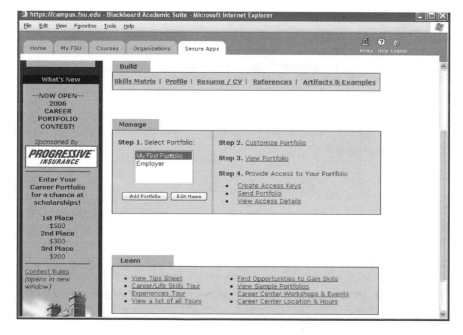

NEW DIRECTIONS FOR STUDENT SERVICES • DOI: 10.1002/ss

Build. Within the build section, students can begin building their skills matrix, profile, résumé or CV, references, and artifacts. Each of these provides an option for an additional tour for students who want more information. Tours provide students with guidance and assistance on an as-needed basis. The remainder of this section provides details about the five methods students can use to build their career portfolio.

The skills matrix is the heart of this online Career Portfolio (see Figure 4.4). In the matrix, students build their portfolio by documenting the experiences that have contributed to the development of the nine skill areas identified above, plus additional skill areas of the student's choice. Each cell within the matrix contains data entry screens that give students a framework for entering information about their skill development. Through the skills matrix, they can access all courses on their academic transcript, as well as service experience on their service transcript, through a link with the university registrar database, and import the information directly to the data entry screens. This feature demonstrates one of the ways the program is integrated with many different academic support services of the university (Reardon, Lumsden, and Meyer, 2004).

Furthermore, the skills matrix can also be used as a planning tool. When looking at their individualized skills matrix, students can quickly see which of the skills they have documented. Each cell of the matrix shows how many items are included for that particular area. Students can work with academic advisers in selecting course work that will help them develop a particular skill. They can talk with career advisers, faculty, and others about additional experiences they can be involved in to develop their skills further.

An important component of this portfolio-building process is that students are asked to reflect on their experiences. They are encouraged to describe specifically how a particular experience led to the development of a career or life skill. This reflective process is valuable for students when they engage in the job search or graduate school application process, because it helps prepare them to market their skills to potential employers or admissions committees. In addition, it helps students understand the value of their experiences, understand the linkages among their experiences, and see how they relate to their future.

Some departments on campus are asking students to add specific skills or competencies related to the goals of the major or department. Students can then document the acquisition of these competencies to show mastery of departmental requirements.

The profile section enables users to present an introduction to their Career Portfolio. It is the first page a referred user will see when viewing a student's online Career Portfolio. The profile allows students to highlight any information that they wish to be shown on this first screen. Students are encouraged to include items such as goals, qualifications, and career objectives.

Figure 4.4. Career Portfolio Skills Matrix

Skills	Experiences				
	Jobs / Internships	Courses	Service / Volunteer Work	Memberships / Activities	Interests / Life Experiences
Communication	Add/Edit (5)	Add/Edit (5)	Add/Edit (3)	Add/Edit (2)	Add/Edit (1)
Creativity	Add/Edit (2)	Add/Edit (4)	Add/Edit (1)	Add/Edit (0)	Add/Edit (1)
Critical Thinking	Add/Edit (2)	Add/Edit (1)	Add/Edit (1)	Add/Edit (2)	Add/Edit (0)
Leadership	Add/Edit (2)	Add/Edit (2)	Add/Edit (1)	Add/Edit (2)	Add/Edit (1)
Life Management	Add/Edit (1)	Add/Edit (0)	Add/Edit (1)	Add/Edit (1)	Add/Edit (2)
Research/Project Development	Add/Edit (1)	Add/Edit (1)	Add/Edit (0)	Add/Edit (0)	Add/Edit (0)
Social Responsibility	Add/Edit (0)	Add/Edit (0)	Add/Edit (1)	Add/Edit (0)	Add/Edit (0)
Teamwork	Add/Edit (1)	Add/Edit (1)	Add/Edit (0)	Add/Edit (0)	Add/Edit (0)
Technical/Scientific	Add/Edit (2)	Add/Edit (0)	Add/Edit (1)	Add/Edit (2)	Add/Edit (1)
Knowledge of Subj Matter [edit]	Add/Edit (0)	Add/Edit (1)	Add/Edit (0)	Add/Edit (0)	Add/Edit (0)
Add Your Own Skills					

The résumé/CV section allows students to upload their résumé or CV directly into the Career Portfolio, where they can also maintain multiple versions of their résumé or CV.

The references section allows students to enter contact information for people who can provide references for them. Students are encouraged to develop and maintain relationships with such persons on campus and in the community.

In the artifacts section, students upload samples of their work in a variety of formats. For example, they may want to include writing samples, Power-Point presentations, research papers, artwork, links to Web sites, video or audio clips, or other artifacts that show the scope and quality of their work. This section can be useful for students to keep track of work they have done throughout their college experience and is the epitome of the term *portfolio*.

Manage.   The manage section of the main menu allows students to customize their Career Portfolios (each user is allowed to have up to three versions of his or her e-portfolio). Because students will be documenting their skills and experiences for an extended length of time (ideally, from freshman to senior year or throughout a graduate program), they may have a

NEW DIRECTIONS FOR STUDENT SERVICES • DOI: 10.1002/ss

large number of items in their portfolio. They can customize each of their three portfolio versions to target specific career objectives or meet departmental requirements. They can choose to show only a subset of the information they have included through the build section or all of it. In addition, they can choose to make available their unofficial academic or service transcripts for others to view.

Through the manage section, students also create access keys (passwords) that allow referred users, such as employers, faculty members, graduate school admissions committees, and parents, to view their Career Portfolio. Students can view their Career Portfolio through the manage section and send e-mails with access information directly to people they want to view the portfolio. Finally, students can track the use of access keys to know if and when referred users have accessed their portfolio.

Learn. The learn section of the main menu allows students to access all of the instructional tours, view sample portfolios, and learn about other services the Career Center offers. Most important, students can access "Find Opportunities to Gain Skills," where they can learn about opportunities on campus and in the community that will help them develop their career and life skills. This section includes links to more than three hundred campus organizations as well as student affairs and academic support offices on campus.

Referred User: View Portfolio. The third selection from the home page of this e portfolio is called Referred User: View Portfolio. In this section, those persons referred by students can access a particular Career Portfolio and examine the information provided there. Tabs across the top of the screen organize the output of a particular Career Portfolio, which first opens to the profile screen, where students have summarized the information they want the referred user to see. By clicking on the tabs, referred users can then view a student's résumé or CV, skills, unofficial transcripts, references, and artifacts—but only those sections that the student has made available for viewing (Reardon, Lumsden, and Meyer, 2005).

Implementation and Integration

When first implementing the Career Portfolio, we recognized the importance of partnering with other university departments and offices. Implementation started with a formal launch event and has continued through various partnerships as well as a contest.

Launch of the FSU Career Portfolio. The FSU Career Portfolio was launched campuswide on April 26, 2002, at a formal reception attended by over 150 faculty, administrators, staff, students, employers, and friends. Rather than focus solely on students, the Career Center targeted faculty, staff, and administrators in marketing the launch event. The rationale was that partnerships with these groups would be critical to the success of the program, as they could continue to promote the system to students year after year. The event attracted local media, and the launch of the CPP was highlighted on the local evening news. In addition, articles were published in the *State,* a bulletin for FSU faculty and staff, as well as the *FSView,* the FSU student newspaper, and the *Tallahassee Democrat,* the local newspaper.

Promotion Through Partnerships with Faculty and Advisers. Besides direct self-help use, students are encouraged to develop their FSU Career Portfolio in the context of various courses, academic advising, career planning classes, outreach presentations, and one-on-one career advising. Each of these interventions involves varied faculty and staff working with students in their respective roles and relationships. Every section of First Year Experience (FYE) classes (approximately sixty sections per year) visits the Career Center and is introduced to the Career Portfolio. Outreach presentations are conducted throughout campus, usually at the request of faculty members or student groups. The Career Portfolio is also introduced during career advising, where students drop in to get assistance with their career planning and employment needs.

Career Portfolio Contest. The Career Center holds a Career Portfolio contest during the fall semester each year to identify high-quality portfolios. The contest helps the center learn about the quality and content of Career Portfolios being created by FSU students. In addition, it increases awareness of the Career Portfolio program to FSU students, faculty, staff, and administration. It also increases awareness among employers and helps the Career Center learn more about employers' attitudes toward using it in evaluating candidates. Scholarships are awarded to the first-, second-, and third-place winners. The Career Center provides the opportunity for a corporation to sponsor the contest, which covers the costs associated with awarding the scholarship prizes.

All contest entries are evaluated using a three-step screening process, with the top ten to twelve e-portfolios making it to the third and final round of judging, which is a thorough review by employers and university administrators who serve as judges. The quality of the submitted portfolios for the past four years has been impressive. Many students included a variety of courses they completed over their college years. In addition, a wide range of work and volunteer experiences was represented by the contest entrants. Furthermore, entrants chose to include many different types of artifacts. Some examples of these artifacts include PowerPoint presentations, statements of purpose, syllabi for courses taught, Web sites designed, audio clips of music performances, and sketches drawn and scanned. (Portions of the winners' Career Portfolios are available at www.career.fsu.edu/portfolio/contestwinners.html. Figure 4.5 shows the first-place winner for 2005.)

The Career Portfolio Contest provides many benefits, including increased promotion efforts of the program across campus, insight into the quality of student e-portfolios, increased awareness of employers, and the opportunity for the Career Center to gather data from the employers regarding their use of the Career Portfolio in evaluating candidates.

**Figure 4.5. First-Place Undergraduate Winner,
2005 Career Portfolio Contest**

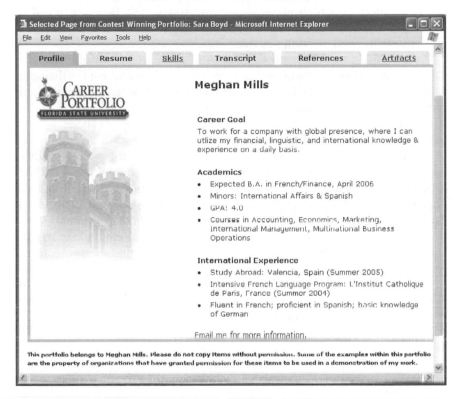

Use of the Career Portfolio

E portfolios are used in various ways to meet the goals of the program, department, or university. The Career Portfolio at FSU was developed with specific goals in mind, but it has been used in ways that were unforeseen at the beginning. We anticipated use of the portfolio in career planning as well as with academic advisers in the planning of students' course work and cocurricular activities. Now that the program has been in place for five years, we have seen other uses that were unanticipated. The CPP has been integrated across the campus and is being used in a variety of ways, including skill identification, planning of course work and cocurricular activities, preparation for marketing in a job or graduate or professional school search, showing professional growth throughout a degree program, providing for reflection and personal development, and as an accreditation tool.

Skills Identification. The Career Portfolio can be useful in helping students learn about important skills that they need to develop, and helping them identify which skills they have and which they still need to develop. Students enrolled in SDS 3340: Introduction to Career Development use the Career Portfolio in this way.

Planning. One of the expected uses of the Career Portfolio was that Career Center advisers would use the program to help students plan their curricular and cocurricular activities. While looking at the skills matrix, students can be encouraged to think about how their classes and outside activities contribute to their skill development and how they can choose classes or other involvement to help them gain desired skills. One living learning community (LLC) at FSU has adopted use of the Career Portfolio in this way. The advisers of the LLC meet with the first-year students and encourage them to think about what they can do to demonstrate the skills incorporated into the Career Portfolio. The director of the program reports that the skills matrix helps students to think about what courses they may want to take or other activities they may want to be involved in to gain or strengthen their skills in the different areas. Academic advisers in the College of Criminology and Criminal Justice are also using the Career Portfolio in this way.

Reflection and Personal Growth. The Career Portfolio can assist students in reflection and attaching meaning to the experiences they are having in college. One program that is using the Career Portfolio in this way is the Freshman Interest Group (FIG) program, implemented by the Division of Undergraduate Studies. Important goals of the FIG program are to help first-time-in-college (FTIC) students understand the value of liberal studies and to connect them in their first semester to the academic culture on campus. The FIG program allows first-year students to register for a cluster of courses linked to a specific theme or program. This enables them to enroll in courses where they will meet other students with similar interests. In addition, students participating in the FIG program are required to enroll in a colloquium course where they learn to reflect on their experiences both in and out of the classroom in order to develop a broader understanding of themselves and their future. FIG colloquiums are taught by upperclassmen who must go through a training course to be FIG leaders. In the training course, these future FIG leaders must complete their Career Portfolio in much the same way that their future freshmen students will (see the chapter appendix). This enables them to fully understand the assignment. The Career Portfolio assignment is done in two installations, and the leaders then must present their portfolios to the instructors and their fellow classmates at the end of the semester. Students are asked to talk about a highlight or significant discovery they made in putting their portfolios together. The dean of undergraduate studies reports that this presentation provokes good dialogue among the students, and some FIG leaders incorporate the presentation of Career Portfolios into their own syllabi with their colloquium group. In addition, the portfolio helps students reflect on their other experiences, such as volunteer work and memberships, and enables them to see that their total experience while at FSU creates the total package to prepare them for the next stage, whatever that may be (K. Laughlin, dean of undergraduate studies, personal communication, November 22, 2006).

A major component of this colloquium course is the completion of the FSU Career Portfolio. By having students start on their Career Portfolio the first semester at FSU, the administrators of the FIG program felt it would help students reflect on the value of the academic work they are doing and enable them to see that their liberal studies course work applies to their academic development and future career goals (Laughlin, personal communication, November 22, 2006). Students are required to build the profile, skills matrix, and artifacts sections of the Career Portfolio and then share it with their FIG leader. They receive feedback from the leader regarding their entries and the quality of their reflection on their experiences. This exercise teaches and encourages students to reflect on their learning experience and helps them to recognize and articulate skills they are developing (Lumsden, Meyer, and Garis, forthcoming).

Karen Laughlin, dean of undergraduate studies, feels that the Career Portfolio is beneficial to the students in several ways. For the FIG leaders, it helps them to pull their work together by looking back to early work and seeing how it all fits together. This can be beneficial in helping students present themselves to others, whether for employment or graduate school. For students planning on graduate school, it can be a helpful tool in preparing to write personal statements and submit to references to help the writer craft a better letter of recommendation and comment more effectively on the student's accomplishments. For the FTIC students, the dean feels that the Career Portfolio creates a powerful lesson for first-year students to help them see that their early course work and other activities are more than just hoops to jump through; there is skill development and learning taking place that will be valuable in the future.

Marketing Tool. Based out of the Career Center, the Career Portfolio has obvious use as a tool for students in marketing themselves in a job search or application to graduate or professional school. Faculty members in a variety of colleges incorporate portfolio building into their class syllabi to help students get started on the process of being able to showcase their skills and accomplishments. All students in human sciences, nursing, higher education (graduate program), theater, English education, and possibly others are required to complete some portion of the Career Portfolio as a class assignment. This enables students to get started on the process and learn the value of completing a portfolio. Portfolio staff members are invited by faculty to present in their classes. Students are also informed of the potential benefits of completing their portfolio, such as being better prepared for interviews and writing personal statements.

Professional Growth. The Career Portfolio allows students to see growth over time. In FSU's School of Theatre, all students must begin their portfolio in their introductory class. They receive feedback on the portfolio and are encouraged to continue adding to it while completing their degree. In their senior-year capstone class, students are required to complete their Career Portfolio and present it to their classmates and faculty. Students are able to see their growth over the course of their program and practice sharing and showcasing themselves.

Accreditation. Another unexpected use of the Career Portfolio has been in support of program and university accreditation efforts. The athletic training program, part of the College of Human Sciences, is accredited by the Commission on Accreditation of Athletic Training Education. One of its standards is professional development and responsibility (http://caate.net/ss_docs/standards.6.8.2006.pdf). To fulfill this requirement, the program director for athletic training gives students an assignment to complete the following parts of the Career Portfolio: upload the résumé, make five entries in the skills matrix, and enter references. She then has them send her a link to view their portfolio, where she checks to see that they have completed this assignment. The program director explains the benefits of using the Career Portfolio. For students, it is beneficial in helping them apply what they learn in the classroom, they can maintain their CP after graduation, graduate school committees find it helpful, and they have the opportunity to individualize their CP through artifacts, and so on. For instructors and the department, the portfolio provides a vehicle for fulfilling professional development criteria. The system was already created so the department did not have to create something new, and the tutorials walk a student through the process. In addition, the program director notes that when a student applies to the athletic training program, she sees it as positive if the student submits the Career Portfolio with his or her admission application (A. Sehgal, personal communication, November 9, 2006).

Another example is the fact that FSU academic administrators have found the Career Portfolio to be a valuable component in the accreditation process. As discussed in Chapter One, FSU is using the Career Portfolio to meet accreditation requirements of the Southern Association of Colleges and Schools.

In order to accommodate specific skills in some disciplines, the FSU Career Portfolio was redesigned to allow students to add skills. As a result, academic departments can direct students to add selected specialized skills as stipulated or required by accrediting boards. Furthermore, students can submit specialized career portfolios that follow accrediting board guidelines to their academic department and faculty for review. The FSU Career Portfolio offers students the opportunity to create up to three versions. Currently, consideration is being given to designing an optional version of a Career Portfolio with the capability for faculty to evaluate and rate student competencies or learning outcomes within the portfolio system. Faculty-rated portfolios could then be submitted to accrediting boards (Lumsden, Meyer, and Garis, forthcoming).

NEW DIRECTIONS FOR STUDENT SERVICES • DOI: 10.1002/ss

Student and Employer Evaluation

The FSU Career Portfolio has undergone several activities aimed at evaluating its effectiveness as a career development tool. Both students and employers provided feedback regarding the CPP, and the evaluation efforts continue to be conducted on an annual basis.

Student Evaluation Results. In 2003, Career Center staff created an online survey in an effort to collect information related to students' perceptions of the Career Portfolio. This survey asks students to rate the program's effectiveness and indicate how they intend to use their portfolio. The online survey is sent electronically to all students, who are required to complete one or more portions of the portfolio as part of a class assignment.

Between 2003 and 2006, surveys were e mailed to students enrolled in a variety of courses, ranging from an undergraduate nursing class to a graduate-level higher education class. Completed surveys were obtained from 446 students. In response to who helped them develop their Career Portfolio, faculty (47 percent) and career advisers working in the Career Center (19 percent) were most frequently mentioned. Twenty-five percent received help from no one. These individuals most likely were able to navigate the system on their own and use the tutorials to build and manage their portfolios.

The survey contained ten items related to the goals of the CPP. Students had the option of strongly agreeing, agreeing, disagreeing, or strongly disagreeing to statements aimed at evaluating the effectiveness of the CPP. Students could also check "not applicable." The majority of students had positive views of the CPP, as this summary shows:

- Seventy-two percent strongly agreed or agreed that the CPP helped them find experiences at FSU that would lead to the development of transferable skills.
- Sixty percent strongly agreed or agreed that the CPP helped them find experiences in the community that would lead to the development of skills.
- Eighty-six percent strongly agreed or agreed that the CPP helped them understand how their academic and professional skills related to personal career goals.
- Eighty-one percent strongly agreed or agreed that the CPP helped them show evidence of interpersonal skills needed to work with or for others.
- Ninety-one percent strongly agreed or agreed that the CPP helped them show evidence of skills developed in their academic program.
- Eighty-eight percent strongly agreed or agreed that the CPP helped them show evidence of skills developed through volunteer experiences, part-time employment, internships, or a cooperative education program.
- Eighty-five percent strongly agreed or agreed that the CPP helped them show evidence of skills that could apply to a variety of occupations.
- Eighty-two percent strongly agreed or agreed that the CPP helped them show evidence of skills necessary to obtain and maintain employment.

• Eighty-seven percent strongly agreed or agreed that the CPP helped them communicate their skills to potential employers.
• Seventy-eight percent strongly agreed or agreed that the CPP helped them prepare for job searching and interviewing.

Students were also asked to indicate how they intended to use their completed Career Portfolio. Besides using it for a class assignment (the most common response), the top three ways students planned to use their Career Portfolio were applying for a job, identifying their skills, or applying for graduate or professional school. The two least frequent uses identified by students were applying for an internship and interview preparation.

Employer Evaluation Results. In addition to the surveys designed for students' feedback, Career Center staff took several opportunities to solicit evaluation data on the Career Portfolio Program from employers. Prior to the launch of the program in April 2002, employers provided input into the design of the system, including which skills were needed most and used most frequently in the workplace, the usefulness of an online career portfolio system in their recruiting efforts, and the usability and effectiveness of the first CPP prototype. After the launch of the FSU Career Portfolio, questions regarding the CPP were added to employer evaluations for career expositions and on-campus recruiting. (A detailed description of all of these early employer surveys can be found in Reardon, Lumsden, and Meyer, 2004.)

With the success of implementing and evaluating the FSU Career Portfolio Program, opportunities arose to make the system available. Efforts to transfer the system to other colleges and universities have been successful.

Transfer of the FSU Career Portfolio to Other Colleges and Universities

Another accomplishment of the FSU Career Portfolio is its adaptation for a statewide system and its adoption by two major universities. Due to these accomplishments, FSU has initiated marketing efforts nationally and internationally.

FACTS Career Portfolio. FSU transferred the Career Portfolio concept, design, and supporting software code for use within Florida to a state-related organization, Florida Academic Counseling and Tracking for Students System (FACTS; www.facts.org). FACTS has a variety of online applications to assist high school, community college, and public university students in applying and transferring to colleges, obtaining academic advising information, learning about financial aid, and accessing academic information and records. One application focused on career planning and, under a licensing agreement with FSU, FACTS created a customized version of the FSU Career Portfolio that is available for use by all community colleges and public universities in Florida.

NEW DIRECTIONS FOR STUDENT SERVICES • DOI: 10.1002/ss

The FACTS version of the Career Portfolio is housed and made available to students and colleges and universities through a server located at the University of South Florida. The FACTS version differs from the original FSU Career Portfolio in several important ways: the system is a generic version and is not customizable by the various institutional users in Florida; the FACTS Career Portfolio is not integrated into the institutions' databases, which prevents students from including an academic transcript or viewing their courses directly while in the system; and other institutionally specific information cannot be included, such as links to specific college, university, and community Web sites.

Although limited as a generic version, the FACTS Career Portfolio has been quite successful and has enjoyed widespread use throughout Florida. Clearly an important factor contributing to the success of the FACTS version is its cost-effectiveness: colleges, universities, and their students have free access to the FACTS Career Portfolio. Furthermore, since it is offered through FACTS, the portfolio and student user are not identified with any specific college or university. As a result, the FACTS portfolio is transferable as students attend new institutions. Through the agreement with FACTS, the FSU Career Portfolio now enjoys widespread accessibility and use by college and university students throughout Florida. From its launch on June 1, 2004, through June 30, 2006, 18,630 FACTS Career Portfolios were created.

Adoption of the FSU Career Portfolio by Other Universities. In considering marketing efforts outside Florida, the FSU Career Center was interested in learning about the transferability of the Career Portfolio to other specific out-of-state institutions. As a result, FSU transferred the Career Portfolio concept, design, and software code at no cost to the University of California, San Diego, and the Georgia Institute of Technology. More information about Career Portfolio implementation and use at these universities can be found in Chapters Five and Six.

NACELink/Symplicity Alliance. Many colleges and universities have contacted FSU to inquire about adapting the program for their use. As part of the NACELink/Symplicity partnership, interested schools will be able to license an e-portfolio based on the FSU model.

Summary

The FSU Career Portfolio is an example of an e-portfolio program developed in-house to meet the goals of the Career Center and the university. Many unanticipated uses have materialized, with the program becoming more integrated into the university through its five-year history. The FSU Career Portfolio is also an example of how e-portfolio programs can provide linkages between student affairs and academic affairs, fostering partnerships that ultimately benefit students.

NEW DIRECTIONS FOR STUDENT SERVICES • DOI: 10.1002/ss

Appendix: FIG Career Portfolio Assignment

Objective. This portfolio assignment will provide you with a structured opportunity to reflect on your own experiences and develop a stronger understanding of who you are as a person at this time. In particular, it will allow you to consider your courses and activities at FSU and the ways these have helped you develop a range of skills and accomplishments. For this assignment, you will also be able to include a few selected experiences from high school in order to give you additional practice in using the portfolio and to help you draw a more complete picture of yourself at this stage of your academic career.

Portfolio Basics. Do you have a place in your home or elsewhere where you keep important documents, pictures or other items that are of significance to you personally, scholastically and/or professionally? If so, you have a portfolio, at least at its most basic level. For some people it's a shoebox, for others it's a filing cabinet, for others it's a binder or scrapbook. The gist is that most people do in fact have a repository for important "stuff" so that they can review and re-organize it from time to time. People often refer to particular elements of their collections of materials when describing themselves to other people, either for recreation or for personal gain (e.g., college or graduate school admission, scholarship applications, job interviews). Putting this material together in a more formal way gives you a chance to reflect on your accomplishments and experiences while looking ahead to the next stage(s) of your life. In sum, three ideas characterize portfolios, at least insofar as we'll use them in the FIG program:

1. When looking at a person's portfolio it describes who s/he is at a particular point in time; a portfolio is a person's personal history and its contents can be observed (by its owner or other people) and analyzed to provide clues regarding the person's experiences, values and perspectives.
2. Portfolios can be used for personal development as well as for presentation to selected audiences for any number of purposes.
3. The three steps for portfolio-building include a continuous, fluid process of "collection," "reflection," and "action." The third step—action—may be an actual presentation to other people or it may be any other sort of action (e.g., particular decisions, dedication to a particular project, development of particular skills, aspirations and goals) that a person takes as a result of having engaged in reflection about his/her life as represented by the collection of things in his/her portfolio.

Though we will be developing career portfolios in the FIG program in some very specific ways, it is important to keep in mind these basic ideas in order to stay focused on the big picture and not get lost in technical details.

The "Portfolio" Tool. To facilitate your portfolio-building experience, we'll be making use of FSU's web-based "Career Portfolio" tool. All faculty, staff and students have access to this tool at http://portfolio.fsu.edu. One note of interest is that there are two sides to the Portfolio tool: the "instructor" (or "referred user") side and the "student" side. You'll be using the "student" side but will be referring your FIG Leader(s) to the "instructor/referred user" side so that they can review and assist you with building your portfolio.

Your Portfolio. You will complete two installments of your portfolio this semester. Each installment will be due on the date indicated on the timeline for your FIG.

Follow these steps to get started:

1. Go to http://portfolio.fsu.edu/, click on the link "FSU Students and Alumni: Enter Portfolio," and log-in with your FSUID and password.
2. Once at the Main Menu, take the tour for First-Time users by clicking on the link in the left sidebar under "First Time User?—Take This Tour!" You might also want to take a look at your FIG Leader's portfolio using the Referred Users link. S/he will give you instructions for accessing this in class.
3. In the "Manage Portfolio" section, set up a new Portfolio entitled "FIG Portfolio" by clicking on the "Add Portfolio" button and typing this in as a new name.

Requirements for First Installment. Begin thinking about how your course work and extracurricular activities at FSU (and before you got here) have helped you develop skills and artifacts that demonstrate your own strengths and interests.

1. In the Profile Section—make at least one entry. This could be any of the following:

- A welcome message
- A statement of your goals
- Some other way(s) you'd like to personalize your portfolio

2. In the Skills Section (make a total of two entries MINIMUM selected from the following):

- Entries for your FSU courses (at least one skill/course).
- Entries for classes you took in high school (these might be dual enrollment, AP, Honors or just regular high school courses—at least one skill/course).
- Entries for additional types of experiences (jobs, service, memberships, interests, etc. (at least one skill for each). You may use experiences from your high school years here, though it's good to include experiences from this first semester at FSU if you can.

3. Add one or more artifacts (at least one for this assignment—preferably an example of work you have done since coming to FSU).

Make sure you include a description of any artifact you include and why it is useful/important to your presentation of yourself. The Career Center can help you upload artifacts if you have difficulties with this.

4. Once you have completed these entries, go into the "Customize Portfolio" link (Step 3 under the Manage section). Turn "on" the entries you want to show in your FIG Portfolio. You may also put the entries in order by using the Ranking function.

5. Create an access key for your FIG Portfolio so the FIG Leader(s) can access your portfolio. You may name it anything you like, using letters or numbers but no spaces. Once this is done COPY your URL. Go to "Send Portfolio," select your access key, and enter the FIG Leader's email address. (This should be on your syllabus.) In the message box, PASTE the URL to your FIG Portfolio. Preview and send.

6. ALSO, please print a copy of your FIG Portfolio (using "View Portfolio") and bring it to class on the date due.

NOTE: If you have other Career Portfolio entries, be sure to use the "Customize Portfolio" function to organize your materials and select each item you want to appear in your FIG Portfolio before you send/print it. *This is a very important step!*

Requirements for Second Installment.

1. Review/revise your entries from the first installment.

2. In the Skills Section: add entries (and/or revise your previous entries as needed) to bring your total entries up to at least five. These should include a mix of classes and out-of-class activities: at least two FSU classes and at least two additional experiences and activities (from this fall or earlier).

3. Add artifacts (or replace your previous one) if you wish.

4. Customize, send and print your portfolio as you did for the first installment.

5. Prepare a brief (approximately one-page) reflection on your portfolio:

- What strengths do you see?
- What skills do you need to develop?
- How have your experiences at FSU so far contributed to the development of your own career/life skills?

Hand this in along with the printed copy of your second installment.

References

Lumsden, J. A., Meyer, K. E., and Garis, J. W. "Development, Implementation, and Evaluation of an e-Portfolio at an American University." In M. Kankaanranta, P. Linnakyla, and J. Kaisto (eds.), *Perspectives on ePortfolios.* Forthcoming.

Lumsden, J. A., and others. "Developing an Online Career Portfolio." *Journal of Career Planning and Employment,* 2001, *62*(1), 33–38.

Reardon, R., Lenz, J., Sampson, J., and Peterson, G. *Career Development and Planning: A Comprehensive Approach.* (2nd ed.) Stamford, Conn.: Thomson Corporation, 2006.

Reardon, R. C., Lumsden, J. A., and Meyer, K. E. "The FSU Career Portfolio Program." Tallahassee: Florida State University, Center for the Study of Technology in Counseling and Career Development, 2004.

Reardon, R. C., Lumsden, J. A., and Meyer, K. E. "Developing an e-Portfolio Program: Providing a Comprehensive Tool for Student Development, Reflection, and Integration." *NASPA Journal,* 2005, *42*(3), 368–380.

JILL A. LUMSDEN *is the career portfolio project coordinator at the Career Center, Florida State University, Tallahassee.*

NEW DIRECTIONS FOR STUDENT SERVICES • DOI: 10.1002/ss

5

This chapter describes the planning, development, testing, and launching phases of UCSD's online career portfolio, as well as a summary of its impact and discussion of its future.

Adaptation of the Career Portfolio at the University of California, San Diego: A Case Study

Andrew Ceperley, Craig Schmidt

In fall 2004, the University of California, San Diego (UCSD) officially launched its own customized version of the online Career Portfolio, originally developed by Florida State University (Lumsden and others, 2001) This launch represented the culmination of nearly sixteen months of planning and development by a multidisciplinary team comprising Career Services Center practitioners, campus technical staff, and Web writers. To some extent, the official approval and subsequent implementation process can be viewed as a confluence of campus factors and events jointly contributing to the perception that this was the right time and UCSD the right place for this important online tool.

There had been previous discussions about the relative merits of implementing an online career portfolio tool at UCSD dating back to the mid-1990s in our Career Services Center management team meetings. Although the general tenor of these discussions was positive, questions about return on investment for developing such a tool and, in particular, concerns as to perceived value by both students and employers, kept any initiative from taking shape. However, with the ongoing trend of an increasingly technologically savvy student population, in conjunction with a series of key campus developments, the idea of an online career portfolio began to gain traction.

NEW DIRECTIONS FOR STUDENT SERVICES, no. 119, Fall 2007 © Wiley Periodicals, Inc.
Published online in Wiley InterScience (www.interscience.wiley.com) • DOI: 10.1002/ss.249

In 2002, the Division of Student Affairs under the direction of its vice chancellor developed the first student affairs strategic plan, intended to be a working document guiding the direction and priorities of UCSD student affairs over the period 2002 to 2007. The strategic plan was developed based on a number of key assumptions, including two that specifically supported the concept of an online career portfolio at UCSD:

- Entering UCSD students will continue to be more technologically savvy and demand technology-based services.
- As technology advances, student service units need to adapt their service delivery mechanisms to meet student demand.

A key objective addressing these assumptions was to develop priorities within student affairs for Web development and enhancement, guided by a philosophy of improving student outcomes. At its foundation was the principle of providing student services with 24/7 access. Out of this broad framework for expanding Web-based technology to support student career outcomes came specific action items such as the development of an e-career advising feature. The timing and availability of the proposed online career portfolio proved serendipitous in relation to this emerging technologically supportive strategic plan.

Another significant campus development that had a positive impact on the implementation of the career portfolio was the creation of a new sixth college, with its inaugural class in fall of 2002. Every undergraduate at UCSD belongs to one of the six colleges, each with its own unique programmatic theme, curricular requirements, and extracurricular student life. This system of colleges at UCSD offers students the best of both worlds: a small liberal arts college environment, along with the advantages of a large research university. The new sixth college, with its programmatic theme emphasizing the relationships of art, culture, and technology, supports the importance of experiential education, enhanced communication skills, and digital competency. The career portfolio's use of technology to help students develop and document their skills and experiences, both curricular and noncurricular, clearly supported the thematic goals of this sixth college.

The potential benefits and complementary nature of this tool did not go unnoticed by sixth college administration. Their new college provost became a strong advocate for career portfolio implementation at a critical time in fall 2002 and provided written support to key decision makers describing how the tool could be integrated into the experiences of sixth college students. This support, coupled with a newly developed student affairs strategic plan that emphasized emerging Web-based technologies, created a campus environment ready to embrace an online career portfolio at UCSD. The unique opportunity to adapt and implement an already developed career portfolio tool such as the one created at Florida State University was well received by the campus Web advisory committee, and with input from the vice chancellor of student affairs, approval was given to make the career portfolio implementation project a top technical priority in spring 2003.

Adapting and Implementing the Career Portfolio at UCSD

Once an agreement was reached with Florida State University regarding the sharing of its Career Portfolio tool and approval was given by the UCSD Web advisory committee to proceed, the process of implementation began in the summer of 2003. This process can be broken into three distinct phases: the planning phase, the development phase, and the testing phase. The overall goal was to adapt and implement the FSU Career Portfolio to work efficiently within the UCSD technical Web environment and also meet the unique career development needs of students. Because the FSU tool was very well researched and developed, the plan was to be judicious with any adaptations, performing only those deemed important to the technical performance or students' understanding and acceptance of the tool.

Planning Phase. The planning phase of this project took place during late summer and early fall 2003 and had these elements:

- Creating a multidisciplinary working committee from key stakeholder departments
- Developing a working project implementation plan with specific goals and time line
- Developing a licensing agreement between UCSD and FSU to clearly articulate expectations and understanding regarding how the Career Portfolio would be used at UCSD

Participation in the Career Portfolio work group was drawn from key campus departments that had a strong buy in for this project: career advising and technical staff from the Career Services Center, a project manager and programmers from the campus academic computing and telecommunications unit, and the electronic student services coordinator for StudentLink, the campuswide one-stop Web portal for student information, where the Career Portfolio would ultimately reside. Campus Web writers would also become involved at a later point to ensure that any text revisions would be Web-friendly. During initial planning meetings, the work group developed a detailed project plan outlining the scope and objectives, benchmarking points with projected completion dates, and other technical considerations. This tool proved to be quite useful in monitoring the group's progress in relation to desired deadlines.

One additional issue was to secure a working site license agreement between the two universities. The Career Portfolio tool was created at FSU with a patent pending at the time of this sharing agreement. UCSD was given permission to adapt and implement the concept, design, and code of this portfolio product in an effort to demonstrate its transferability to other institutions. Developing an agreement as to the extent of the adaptations and subsequent use of the tool was handled with the expertise of both institutions' technology transfer departments.

Development Phase. With a work group in place and detailed project plan developed, the task of adapting the Career Portfolio to UCSD began in earnest. While the FSU Career Portfolio provided an outstanding, well-developed platform, there remained four key challenges to address in order to adapt it to the UCSD environment:

1. Review the content and functionality of the various features of the Career Portfolio to ensure the tool would positively resonate with our user population.
2. Adapt the code to allow the software to function efficiently in the UCSD technical environment. This task would involve telecollaboration with technical staff from both universities.
3. Refine the overall visual appearance to give our version of the Career Portfolio the look and feel of UCSD (our "decorator").
4. Adapt the application to make it as portable as possible to demonstrate that it could be packaged and installed at other universities.

Over the course of the next eight months, a series of weekly meetings with the Career Portfolio work group took place to review each section and determine if any modifications were needed. This process required periodic subgroup meetings to review and customize specific features for our students. For example, although the original FSU portfolio provided excellent examples of skills, accomplishments, and experience descriptions in the skills matrix, they tended to be specific to FSU students. To address this issue, a subgroup of career advisers reviewed all of the examples in the skills section and revised them to include experiences that more closely reflected those of UCSD students. In addition, the resources in the Opportunities for Practical Experience section needed to be replaced with UCSD-specific possibilities.

From a technical standpoint, the Career Portfolio had to work within our Java framework, specifically running in a J2EE environment. We needed it to be integrated with our current student sign-on, use our internally developed methods for communicating with the main student information database, and give it the look and feel of UCSD. Web pages were rewritten to create the user interface and separate it from the database. These pages included the implementation of features to retrieve and update specific data, including retrieving information from our student system for displaying courses completed. This design made the application more portable and flexible, potentially allowing other universities to incorporate their own data access methods into the program without modifying the basic presentation. Because this was written as a J2EE Java application, we were able to use filters to incorporate several features of our environment into the application while allowing us to isolate these environment-specific functions. Our log-in security, session management, and decorator were all implemented through these filters.

As the work group neared completion of the adaptation process, a team of Web writers from BLINK, the UCSD campus portal, was brought in to assist in the final editing process to ensure that any new content was written in a Web-friendly style that would encourage student understanding and use.

Testing Phase. As the technical and content adaptations neared completion in the summer of 2004, the next phase was to test the program with student groups prior to the official launch in the fall. To that end, two student focus groups of ten students each were organized and given access to the prototype of the Career Portfolio in the Career Services Center Online Career Lab. These groups, with minimal direction, were asked to go into the tool and create their own portfolios using the First Time User instructional page and More Info screens provided in the tool. Essentially we encouraged students to try to "break" it and then provide us with feedback of their impressions. This process confirmed the effectiveness of the adaptation process and provided additional feedback to fine-tune both the program itself and the online user instructions. After a few minor adjustments, the Career Portfolio was ready for its planned fall 2004 launch.

Launching the Career Portfolio at UCSD

As we set out to launch the Career Portfolio, we considered its unique position within the Career Services Center's mix of services and programs. The portfolio connected student self-assessment during the early college years with the job or graduate school application process during the senior year. To be successful, the portfolio needed to be central in our marketing strategy to students.

As we devised our initial marketing plan, we were thoughtful in matching the portfolio's value with the characteristics exhibited by today's students, dubbed the millennials. Like students on other campuses, UCSD students demonstrate the following personal traits:

- They are sophisticated users of technology.
- They are comfortable with and seek out group activities that will build their credentials.
- They pursue internships to provide them a competitive edge.
- They are impatient in their pursuit of career ambitions.
- They are accustomed to experiencing success.

The launch challenge was to capture these millennial themes in our messages to first-year students and identify opportunities to repeat the message throughout their UCSD careers. In addition, it proved essential to identify and pursue a variety of campus partnerships to broaden the message through repetition from parents, academic advisers, student life officials, and faculty.

By slightly reshaping the structure of our career counseling staff, we were able to craft an online career resources coordinator position. In addition to day-to-day counseling, this new professional was tasked with building out and promoting any Web-related tools and resources, such as online industry directories, interview tutorials, and self-assessment tools; approximately 30 percent of her job is dedicated to these initiatives. An example of a marketing flyer developed for UCSD students is shown in Figure 5.1.

The marketing message we developed and have maintained throughout the portfolio's first two years at UCSD uses the image of a compass and asks students to "position yourself for career success." The message highlights five actions students can take within their personal online portfolio space:

• Learn about opportunities to gain experience on campus and in the community.
• Identify skills that are valued by today's employers.
• Track your experience in nine marketable skill areas.
• Showcase qualifications.
• Create, customize, and store up to three different portfolios and share them only with those you choose.

The message and tag line appeared in fliers, large campus posters, newspaper ads, and a PowerPoint presentation. The following strategies were applied to build awareness of the Career Portfolio:

• Career Services Center open house presentations
• Special student portfolio workshops
• Cross-marketing with other programs
• Outreach to student leadership organizations
• Information sessions with college advising staff
• Parent orientations and online newsletter

Easy access to the Career Portfolio proved beneficial as our launch was timed with the buildup of the new student portal, TritonLink. Career Portfolio is a featured tab on the student desktop and can be accessed through their personal ID and access code.

Progress and Continued Evolution

As of September 2006, 11,669 students have created Career Portfolios. Portfolio creation among the six undergraduate colleges is balanced. Although the vast majority of students create just one portfolio, we have noticed a growth in the percentage of students customizing two and even three portfolios. As promising as UCSD's early statistics may be, we acknowledge that

Figure 5.1. UCSD Portfolio Student Flyer

Keep track of it all in one convenient place!

Online Career Portfolio

A Career Portfolio helps you:

- **Stay organized...**
  by storing your key information in digital form

- **Track your experience...**
  in nine marketable skill areas

- **Identify skills...**
  that are valued by employers and graduate schools

- **Breeze through applications...**
  because your vital information is in one location

- **Discover new opportunities...**
  to strengthen your resume and gain skills

Build up to three different personal, customized portfolios that you can share with others, including potential employers. Forget those overflowing file folders—use the Portfolio to track your:

- Resumes and professional references
- Work samples (writing, websites, presentations, projects)
- Courses and trainings
- Paid and volunteer work experience
- Memberships and organizational activities
- Life experiences (sports, travel, language abilities)

Questions? Talk with an advisor at the Career Services Center or visit career.ucsd.edu for more information

What UCSD students are saying:

It's nice to have one tool to hold all my information, especially my writing samples.
— Senior, Political Science

The skills matrix element is a wonderful tool to help round out my marketable skills, by showing the areas that I still need to work on.
— Junior, Linguistics

I like the fact that you can send the portfolio to potential employers.
— Senior, Computer Science

To use Career Portfolio:
1. Go to tritonlink.ucsd.edu
2. Click on 'Career Portfolio'
3. Log on with your PID/PAC
4. Read the 'First-Time User' information and get started!

A Department of Student Affairs
Career Services Center
University of California, San Diego

On Library Walk
858.534.3750
career.ucsd.edu

our emphasis to date has been the creation of portfolios. But the tool's success over time will hinge on students' regular, continuous use. As a developmental tool, the portfolio should grow as a student grows during the college years. Students should be working with their Career Portfolios every

NEW DIRECTIONS FOR STUDENT SERVICES • DOI: 10.1002/ss

academic term and drawing from them to prepare for interviews and share with interested parties, such as employers, parents, and advisers. The portfolio's utility should include major selection, academic planning, and skill development.

We are confident that good timing will propel the Career Portfolio into its second two years on our campus. Our growing student career peer educator program will provide an additional student-to-student promotional opportunity. The continued collection of quotations from students, alumni, and employers will showcase successful outcomes. In the spring of 2007, UCSD opened its new state-of-the-art academic services building, housing together for the first time core student services, such as admissions, registrar, and bursar. The opening coincided with a student affairs emphasis of providing online 24/7 access to pertinent student tools and resources; the Career Portfolio fits well into this campaign.

A few months before writing of this chapter, we established a Career Services Center task force to improve awareness of students, staff, and faculty and increase both student portfolio creation and, especially, updating and sending. The task force draws from all units in our twenty-eight-person center, including career counseling, graduate and professional school advising, student employment, and marketing. They will work to develop five specific initiatives and measurable benchmarks to be submitted to the Career Services Center's executive management team.

In the initial meeting of the task force, we clarified core users in two levels: new students (both first year and transfers) and upper-division students. We also identified our primary and secondary stakeholders. Primary stakeholders are Career Services Center staff, student affairs colleagues, and provosts, advisers, and faculty members in academic affairs. Secondary stakeholders are employer and graduate school admissions officials.

As we move ahead with concepts to institutionalize the Career Portfolio, we do so with great optimism about this contemporary online tool that is already demonstrating its power to help students make sense of their college experiences, learn from them, and position them for future professional pursuits.

Reference

Lumsden, J. A., and others. "A Blueprint for Building an Online Career Portfolio." *Journal of Career Planning and Employment,* 2001, 62(1), 33–38.

ANDREW CEPERLEY *is the director of the Career Services Center at the University of California, San Diego.*

CRAIG SCHMIDT *is assistant director of the career development programs unit of the Career Services Center at the University of California, San Diego.*

6

This chapter describes the planning, development, testing, and implementation of Georgia Tech's online career port-folio, as well as the challenges associated with adaptation of the program.

Adaptation of a Career Portfolio at Georgia Tech: A Case Study

Ralph Mobley

In January 2002 during a student leadership retreat, a group of Georgia Tech student leaders raised the issue of cocurricular transcripts. These students wanted a way to document and keep track of their leadership, volunteer, and other extracurricular activities. At the time, GT EDGE, a program within the dean of students' office that was designed to capture certain cocurricular activities such as career-related seminars, leadership workshops, and diversity seminars, had ceased to be viable, and students and administrators were looking for a replacement.

Also during this time period, *leadership* had become an often-heard word both on campus and off. Discussions about student leadership development and programming, then as now, were occurring within various departments and student organizations on campus. Within student affairs a great deal of work had gone into defining "pillars of leadership" for students. These pillars were intended to illuminate key aspects of leadership and were intended to form the basis for creating programs and opportunities for student leadership training and experiences.

The concept of pillars was later abandoned; however, in this environment, the idea of a cocurricular transcript quickly evolved into what became known as the Leadership Portfolio. The discussions revolved tightly around the emerging plans for leadership education, building student awareness of leadership principles, and the ability for students to document and track leadership activities.

NEW DIRECTIONS FOR STUDENT SERVICES, no. 119, Fall 2007   © Wiley Periodicals, Inc.
Published online in Wiley InterScience (www.interscience.wiley.com) • DOI: 10.1002/ss.250

The vice president of student affairs had heard of the Florida State University (FSU) Career Portfolio, and this served as the e-portfolio initiative at Georgia Tech. As a result, the career services offices at Georgia Tech and FSU communicated regarding a possible collaborative effort in redesigning the FSU Career Portfolio system at Georgia Tech.

Access was granted to the FSU system, and it was demonstrated to a group of administrators and students at Georgia Tech. Although initial reactions were positive, Georgia Tech staff and faculty were not aware if alternative programs were available and lacked data regarding the quality of such alternative programs if they existed. As a result, a review of other potential e-portfolio systems was conducted.

This review began a lengthy process of looking at other online portfolio possibilities in use at other universities around the country, as well as commercially available offerings. Naturally each of the systems considered had strengths and weaknesses. Some were best suited for classroom use as a basis for assessing learning objectives, others offered excellent journaling features, and still others offered advantages such as simplicity of use. In the end, we determined that the FSU system was best suited to Georgia Tech for several reasons. We liked the student focus of Career Portfolio, particularly since this was a student-initiated idea. There was some sentiment that any portfolio system we adopted or developed should be designed to deliver assessment data and be closely linked with efforts to better quantify and define assessment initiatives within student affairs. Student needs remained the primary focus, and ultimately we agreed that although assessment initiatives were valuable for faculty and administrators, they must not become the overriding goal of the portfolio. In addition, we liked the ease of use of the system. It appeared that students would need little, if any, training or staff support to use the FSU model. This was a substantial benefit because no budget or staff existed to provide training. Also, we were particularly interested in the skills matrix included in the FSU Career Portfolio. Simple in execution and elegant in concept, it offered a launching point from which students could easily use and understand the system.

Development

Through communication with the FSU Career Center and Office of Technology Transfer, Georgia Tech was provided with rights to the FSU Career Portfolio concept, design, and software code free of charge. Because this would be an application available to all enrolled students, the Enterprise Solutions Division of the Office of Information Technology (OIT) would be the technical developers and stewards of the portfolio at Georgia Tech. It quickly became clear that OIT did not share the enthusiasm for free software. After reviewing the program, OIT determined it could not support it, meaning the FSU portfolio was written in a language, JAVA applets, for which Georgia

Tech's IT staff had little expertise. The proposed solution was to build the Georgia Tech system from scratch based on the FSU model and using different development tools such as Coldfusion. This potentially meant tremendous expense and project delays for the Division of Student Affairs.

New Leadership. In the midst of the e-portfolio project, the vice president of student affairs retired and the dean of students became the interim vice president. Initially, in terms of the project, this was not a bad turn of events. After all, the dean of students' office had hosted the student leadership retreat, where the e-portfolio issue was initially raised, and the dean had been closely involved from the outset. As a result, the interim vice president chose to set aside money in support of the e-portfolio project in the budget.

With funding approved for the upcoming new fiscal year (2004–05) negotiations continued with OIT, and a time frame for starting the project, a time line for completion, and assignment of responsibilities were developed.

Along with the new fiscal year, a new vice president arrived, and with new leadership came new priorities and a close review of the budget. Questions included, "Why is so much money set aside for this portfolio? What is it, and why is an portfolio necessary? How does this project compare with overall priorities?" These were opinions and questions any new executive would express and ask. In rather short order, it became clear the new vice president for student affairs felt there were more pressing priorities than the online portfolio.

Many discussions and meetings subsequently took place, and the core group that had been working on the project became concerned it was nearing the end of the line. The career services office was in a selling mode with the vice president and became the catalyst in trying to complete the project. While this was happening, negotiations centering on cost continued with OIT.

Three things ultimately came together that enabled the project to go forward. First was OIT's recognition of the potential of the portfolio, particularly by the director of the enterprise systems group. The director liked it and wanted to build it. Second, e-portfolios were starting to garner more attention from student affairs professionals nationally and also within the state of Georgia. Kennesaw State University's career office had developed a system that was getting some attention from the Georgia Board of Regents, and there was growing external evidence, expressed in journal articles and in other ways, validating the value of these systems. Third, as a result of nearly weekly meetings among career services staff, the vice president for student affairs, and other student affairs staff to discuss the merits of the system, the vice president and division eventually came to be a strong and pivotal supporter. The culminating event that supported the e-portfolio project again was when the vice president of student affairs scheduled a meeting with the institute's chief information officer to resolve the issue of cost. Behind the scenes, the director of enterprise systems had been lobbying for doing this project at significantly reduced or no cost. The net result was that if we were willing to wait a few months, OIT would create the software at no cost and maintain it as a standard system, much like existing software products that were already being managed, with no annual fees required from student affairs. This was truly great news.

Writing the Requirements. The original e-portfolio idea was communicated by student leaders to staff within the dean of students' office, and the initial discussion was between and among those students and staff. It was perhaps a year later before Career Services was involved. Ultimately a small e-portfolio project team began to form that consisted of the senior associate dean of students, the director of success programs, and the director of career services.

As plans began to firm up, the e-portfolio project team evolved and expanded to include functional and technical subgroups. The functional team was responsible for defining the system and specifications, creating the content, communicating requirements, and guiding implementation, including marketing. The technical team took guidance from the functional group in order to build it and keep the functional team grounded in reality.

From the outset, student input was sought. Students originated the idea, were involved in the decision to use the FSU model, and were asked for their thoughts at virtually all points along the way. Their comments were especially critical as the system requirements and specifications were being defined. We presented the FSU system to many groups of students, including the undergraduate and graduate student government, classes, and occasionally individual students whose opinion we valued. We asked for feedback from them on functionality, content, text, and the look and feel of the system.

These student forums resulted in several consistent messages. The most important of these, expressed almost universally, was that students wanted a way to capture the information within the skills matrix in order to create a résumé, a feature missing from the FSU Career portfolio. They insisted that for Georgia Tech students to invest significant time in developing portfolios, there had to be an additional concrete result in the development of a résumé.

The résumé requirement could not be ignored, but we had to make a decision. Building a résumé component into the system would require significant additional technical development time, and we had already suffered several significant delays due to leadership changes and funding uncertainties. Our group was feeling the pressure to produce. We debated whether to go ahead with the production schedule and add the résumé function as a phase two enhancement or to substantially delay, by at least a semester, the release of the portfolio. The decision came down to meeting student expectations and answering a simple question: If released without the résumé component, would students use it? We decided the answer was no.

Not Much to Change

It is a testament to the FSU system that there were no fundamental changes made to the skills matrix, despite the fact that no other portion of the portfolio system received nearly the level of scrutiny as the skills matrix. In meetings

NEW DIRECTIONS FOR STUDENT SERVICES • DOI: 10.1002/ss

with students and faculty, you could almost see the mental struggle on their faces as they thought, *Are there more than nine basic skills? There have to be!*

We did rewrite all of the skill and experience definitions to make them more directly applicable to Georgia Tech and to include specific examples from student life. In fact, only two changes of significance were made to the skills matrix. First, a scholarship experience was added in order to give graduate students a place to better delineate and describe their teaching and research experiences and complement the institute's growing focus on undergraduate research. Second, one skill, life management, was expanded to professional development and life management. Georgia Tech students did not see life management as a skill and viewed the concepts discussed there as being too "sophomoric." Conversely, faculty and staff felt many of students could use considerable skill building in this area. Ultimately including professional development in the skills matrix seemed to be a good compromise. Some might ask whether professional development is an experience rather than a skill. However, when viewed from the context of seeking continuous or life-long learning, we determined professional development to indeed be a skill.

Getting the Right Team

The team guiding the development of the system was composed of a functional and a technical subgroup. Overall leadership of the team devolved to me, with assistance from a project director assigned by the OIT. The role of the project director was to communicate the requirements of the functional team to the programmers building the system. Herein lay, as we were to later discover, a fundamental flaw in our organization. Although the functional team met weekly to review progress, discuss changes, and plan the rollout strategy, the technical team was behind the scenes, and only the project director, who was not a programmer, was present at functional meetings. The project director did an excellent job of creating our requirements and keeping us on task for certain deadlines. However, the flaw was having essentially one person communicating the functional team issues to the technical team. The failure to have at least one truly technical person in the weekly functional meetings led to critical misunderstandings of requirements, which led to delays and unnecessary rework on the part of the programmers.

Once representatives from the technical team, who possessed a deep understanding of the development tools and their capability, began attending the meetings, communications and understanding of the systems requirements, although not flawless, certainly improved.

What's in a Name?

The portfolio came from a student leadership initiative and was closely connected to leadership efforts taking place within student affairs. The working name of the system quickly became the "Leadership Portfolio," but over time this name proved to be more problematic. Was the Leadership Portfolio only for student leaders? Of course not, but would the title cause students who did not perceive themselves as leaders to shy away? Was the title somehow elitist? What is the definition of student leadership anyway? Is it a titled position? Is it demonstrating situational leadership without benefit of title? What do students think about it? There was no consensus, but there certainly was confusion. Is the main reason to complete a portfolio to help get a job? students asked. Certainly it is a big reason for most, and as a result, the career elements of the system came to the forefront and the leadership aspects began to be muted. So, what do we call Georgia Tech's e-portfolio? We contemplated Career and Leadership Portfolio, trying to emphasize both aspects. However, that was considered too wordy. Career Portfolio was the FSU name and we did not want to copy it verbatim. Was not part of the reason for this whole thing to give students a way to document cocurricular activities? In essence, was it to be a tool to help students document, along with the academic transcript, their "career" at Georgia Tech? As a result, the system was titled CareerTech, expressed as a single word implying both a student's "career" while at Georgia Tech and his or her career following graduation.

Marketing

Marketing was a primary focus and a topic we discussed regularly from the beginning. We knew we could build an impressive system, but if students did not know about and did not use it, we would have wasted our time and money. Naturally, our funds were limited for this, and we wanted to make the biggest impact for the fewest dollars. As of this writing, the marketing plan is being executed at Georgia Tech, so it is not possible to assess its level of success; however, from the outset, there were two primary short-term goals. One was to focus on incoming freshmen, and the second was to look for ways to embed the portfolio into the fabric of everyday student life.

We focused on freshmen because of consistent comments from students during the development stages—comments like, "I wish I'd had this years ago because I can't remember all the things I've done!" and "As a senior about to graduate, it's daunting to go back and capture all the things I've done here." These led to the belief that encouraging entering students to use the system was an important step in having the portfolio serve as a useful tool for students throughout their Georgia Tech careers. It would enable them to consistently keep up with their activities as they progressed in school.

Elements of the freshman marketing plan included:

- Presentations at summer freshman orientation sessions
- Booths at the marketplace component of orientation, where students and parents could discuss and pick up information about various campus programs and activities

- Building portfolio writing into the curriculum of GT 1000, the university life class all freshmen are encouraged to take
- Communications and demonstrations to academic advisers and other staff closely connected to incoming students to get them enthusiastic and asking students to take advantage of the program

The other primary focus was to build CareerTech into the fabric of student life. However, we came from the realization that it is easy to get freshmen to use the system as part of a class assignment, but it is less easy to get them to keep using it. Our partial solution to the problem was to introduce the CareerTech portfolio as part of the selection process for certain leadership positions. By requiring submission of completed portfolios for leadership positions, students seeking these positions are made aware of the system.

Lessons Learned

Since the initial 2002 concept of designing an e-portfolio at Georgia Tech, the CareerTech system was indeed initiated during summer 2006. Exhibit 6.1 provides a time line that chronicles the project development and summarizes the strengths and challenges associated with the development of CareerTech. This effort had a number of successes. It:

- Kept a student focus and involvement of students throughout the process.
- Brought together a diverse team from within student affairs and OIT with these key representatives: dean of students, director of leadership education and programs, director of student involvement, associate director of OIT enterprise systems, OIT program director, student affairs program manager for information technology, and director of career services. Additional input was provided by the vice president of student affairs, the chief information officer, and the director of the OIT Enterprise Systems.
- Hired a professional writer-editor to maintain a consistent tone throughout the system.
- Maintained constant attention through weekly meetings of the function team.
- Used Georgia Tech's internal communications group to develop marketing and branding images. A tag line was developed for our marketing campaign: "Got a Life? Back It Up!"
- Acquired staff and faculty buy-in through presentations and demonstrations at the associate dean's regular meeting, the undergraduate curriculum director's meeting, academic advisers network meeting, and many more.

And of course there are always improvements to be made and recommendations:

Exhibit 6.1. Time Line for the Development and Implementation of the Georgia Tech e-Portfolio System

January 2002.   Students leaders express desire for cocurricular transcript, later called the "Leadership Portfolio" and ultimately CareerTech.

July 2003.   Vice president asks about FSU system, and career services contacts FSU requesting information about Career Portfolio.

December 2003.   Vice president for student affairs retires and dean of students becomes interim.

Early to mid 2004.   OIT reviews FSU software; student affairs team studies alternative systems.

March 2004.   OIT declines to use FSU software and delivers first estimate to build and maintain portfolio from scratch.

April 2004.   Interim vice president provides funding for 2004–2005 fiscal year.

July 2004.   New VPSA arrives and sets new priorities; funding is jeopardized.

September 2004.   OIT delivers significantly lower project cost estimate; however, cost remains major concern.

January 2005.   VPSA and CIO meet, resulting in agreement that OIT will create portfolio as an institute priority with no technical development funding required from student affairs. Requires waiting six months for OIT to complete other projects.

April 2005.   Portfolio team begins weekly meetings, OIT project director assigned, letter of understanding between OIT and VPSA written and signed.

August 2005.   Functional system specifications are published.

September 2005 to January 2006.   Team writes and edits content with particular focus on skill and experience definitions within the skills matrix. Reviews functions as they are created; provides feedback to the technical team via project liaison.

January 2006.   Concept presented to Student Leader Retreat. Same group originated the idea four years earlier. At this meeting a March 2006 delivery is promised.

January 2006.   Misunderstandings between functional and technical subgroup are uncovered that would cause significant delays in production. This results in including additional technical members in team meetings, including associate director of OIT ES and an OIT programming manager, to improve communications and eliminate misunderstandings.

February through June 2006.   Undertake a stringent review of systems, test functions, involve students in beta testing, redesign and rebuild resume function. The concept and beta version of CareerTech are presented to various staff and faculty audiences including academic advisors, undergraduate coordinators, associate deans, auxiliary services, student affairs, and admissions officers.

NEW DIRECTIONS FOR STUDENT SERVICES • DOI: 10.1002/ss

Exhibit 6.1. (*continued*)

March through July 2006.   Begin to execute marketing plans. Work with internal communication and public relations group; design and develop advertising materials.

May through mid August 2006.   Hire graduate assistant to aid in marketing strategy development and implementation.

July 9, 2006.   Official launch of CareerTech at the first freshman orientation session.

- Have a better organizational relationship between the functional and technical teams. Some major misunderstandings could have been avoided and the technical team may have more quickly and more thoroughly gained an understanding of the overall project concepts and goals had they been more involved in discussions from the outset.
- Acquire more focused attention from the technical team. Often during the project, the programmers were called to handle emergencies and work on other priorities. This interrupted the flow of the project and may have impeded communications to some degree. Momentum was seemingly lost on several occasions.
- Move more expeditiously. This was a slow process, made even slower by some unavoidable obstacles such as changing leadership. Also, adding the résumé template somewhat late in the process delayed the project considerably. Perhaps we could have done a better job of getting system requirements prepared in a timelier manner.
- Consider information security. This became an issue, and the registrar's office became involved unexpectedly regarding student data, specifically transcripts. We should have had conversations with the information security professionals in OIT prior to this concern.

RALPH MOBLEY is director of career services at the Georgia Institute of Technology, Atlanta.

7

This chapter provides a description of the various types of e-portfolios, a discussion of program development considerations, and an overview of e-portfolio evaluation models.

Program Evaluation of e-Portfolios

Robert C. Reardon, Sarah Lucas Hartley

The e-portfolio phenomenon has been likened to a massive technology wave hitting the wide beaches of higher education (Ayala, 2006). A review of the literature suggests that this wave might change the landscape of the beach, washing away existing landmarks and creating a new topography. Moreover, the claims of a beneficial impact on students and the work of student affairs professionals are frequently stated. Some have gone so far as to claim the existence of a general usefulness of e-portfolios and that they have a greater potential to change higher education than any other known technology (Batson, 2002). (One wonders if this includes chalk and a blackboard.) Ironically, Ayala noted that he reviewed three hundred articles and found that fewer than 5 percent provided any data from students about the impact of a portfolio program. The mantra of "e-portfolios are good and good e-portfolios are even better" can be heard throughout the land.

This matter of the impact of e-portfolios is one that would benefit from attention by student affairs professionals because the actual evidence of such claims appears limited. Our survey of the literature revealed one article published in a refereed student affairs journal that included student feedback on an e-portfolio system (Reardon, Lumsden, and Meyer, 2005). Clearly there is much work to be done to substantiate the claims for the success of e-portfolio programs.

In this chapter, we define an e-portfolio program as a planned sequence of learning experiences designed to develop knowledge, skills, and attitudes that enable students to make informed decisions about study or work or to demonstrate learning accomplishments. As a programmatic intervention

NEW DIRECTIONS FOR STUDENT SERVICES, no. 119, Fall 2007   © Wiley Periodicals, Inc.
Published online in Wiley InterScience (www.interscience.wiley.com) • DOI: 10.1002/ss.251

and viewed from a social systems perspective, an e-portfolio program includes a technology-based intervention, varied staff with a wide range of skills, a plan for marketing the e-portfolio to students and other stakeholders, computer and technology support, counseling and teaching personnel to help students reflect on learning experiences and material for inclusion in the portfolio, and a plan for evaluating the e-portfolio program.

This definition means that an e-portfolio program has both programmatic goals and learner outcome objectives that can be measured. The e-portfolio, then, becomes both a treatment (an independent, input variable) and an output (a dependent variable) from the standpoint of research design or program evaluation. As a treatment, the e-portfolio could be considered a purposive intervention that is manipulated by the program developer or the student user. As an output variable, the e-portfolio could be considered the result of a treatment intervention. In e-portfolios, both characteristics are present, and this adds some complexity to the notion of e-portfolio evaluation. Evaluation of an e-portfolio program could focus on the input or output variables, or both.

Such an examination of e-portfolios as described above is missing in the literature. Indeed, a Google search of the terms *evaluation* and *portfolio* reveals articles describing a portfolio as an assessment tool for evaluating an individual or an organization, criteria for evaluating a portfolio, qualities or characteristics of a "good" portfolio, and techniques for grading a portfolio. Such work does not inform us about how an e-portfolio program as a planned sequence of learning experiences would develop student knowledge, skills, and attitudes that demonstrate learning.

Objective-Based Program Development and Evaluation

If learning outcomes or objectives are the focus of an e-portfolio program evaluation, how does one go about identifying potential objectives? In our view, there are several potential sources of such learner outcome objectives. For example, the National Association of Student Personnel Administrators (NASPA) and the American College Personnel Association (ACPA) have adopted such objectives in *Learning Reconsidered,* and other objectives can be found in the Council for the Advancement of Standards in Higher Education and the National Career Development Guidelines.

Learning Reconsidered. In *Learning Reconsidered* (National Association of Student Personnel Administrators and American College Personnel Association, 2004), NASPA and ACPA identified seven student learner outcomes that take a holistic view of the impact of the total college experience and can provide a basis for evaluating an e-portfolio program:

1. Cognitive complexity
2. Knowledge acquisition, integration, and application
3. Humanitarianism

New Directions for Student Services • DOI: 10.1002/ss

4. Civic engagement
5. Interpersonal and intrapersonal competence
6. Practical competence
7. Persistence and academic achievement

These outcome statements include additional details and examples of learning experiences that enable practitioners to develop and evaluate programs in relation to these learner outcomes.

CAS Standards. The Council for the Advancement of Standards in Higher Education (CAS; 2006) was established in 1979 and is a consortium of thirty-five professional associations concerned with the development and use of standards and guidelines for student learning in institutions of higher education. The CAS standards outline relevant learning and development outcome domains on which career services programs should be based: intellectual growth, effective communication, realistic self-appraisal, enhanced self-esteem, clarified values, career choices, leadership development, healthy behaviors, meaningful interpersonal relationships, independence, collaboration, social responsibility, satisfying and productive lifestyles, appreciation of diversity, spiritual awareness, and achievement of personal and educational goals.

National Career Development Guidelines. Given that some e-portfolio programs are focused in the career services area, National Career Development Guidelines (NCDG) standards provide learner outcome criteria for evaluating such programs. (These guidelines can be found at http://www.acrnetwork.org/ncdg.htm.) Domains, goals and indicators organize the NCDG framework. The three domains of Personal Social Development (PS), Educational Achievement and Lifelong Learning (ED), and Career Management (CM) describe content. Under each domain are goals (eleven in total) that define broad areas of career development competency.

Personal Social Development Domain
1. Develop understanding of self to build and maintain a positive self-concept.
2. Develop positive interpersonal skills including respect for diversity.
3. Integrate growth and change into your career development.
4. Balance personal, leisure, community, learner, family, and work roles.

Educational Achievement and Lifelong Learning Domain
5. Attain educational achievement and performance levels needed to reach your personal and career goals.
6. Participate in ongoing, lifelong learning experiences to enhance your ability to function effectively in a diverse and changing economy.

Career Management Domain
7. Create and manage a career plan that meets your career goals.
8. Use a process of decision making as one component of career development.

9. Use accurate, current, and unbiased career information during career planning and management.
10. Master academic, occupational, and general employability skills in order to obtain, create, maintain, and/or advance your employment.
11. Integrate changing employment trends, societal needs, and economic conditions into your career plans.

Under each goal in the framework are indicators of mastery that highlight the knowledge and skills needed to achieve that goal. Each indicator is presented in three learning stages derived from Bloom's Taxonomy: knowledge acquisition, application, and reflection. The stages describe learning competency. They are not tied to an individual's age or level of education.

National Association of Colleges and Employers Professional Standards. The NACE Professional Standards for Colleges and Universities (2006) were updated during 2006, and a technology section was added. Career portfolios are addressed in this section's statements. Also, a NACE standards program evaluation workbook is available to conduct career services self-reviews. The technology section of the workbook parallels the standards and includes an item in support of career portfolios.

Mission and Philosophy

In evaluating an e-portfolio program, it is important to be as clear as possible about the meaning, purpose, and values of the program. This is typically reflected in the mission statement. An example of the kind of mission or guiding philosophy statement that we envision was reported by Reardon and Lumsden (2003). Their statement sets out four principles with related program or learner outcomes:

1. Develop students' strategic career visions. The online career portfolio program should enable students to develop and pursue a strategic career vision.
2. Prepare qualified graduates. The university should be dedicated to producing graduates who are needed in an emerging global economy that is characterized by lean production, information technology, and alternative ways of working (Reardon, Lenz, Sampson, and Peterson, 2000).
3. Provide evidence of student preparation. The career-portfolio program should provide employers of college graduates with evidence that students are ready to make effective contributions in the workplace.
4. Link education, work, and community. The career portfolio program, focusing on life and career preparation, should link education and employment and provide connections between education, work, and community organizations.

Figure 7.1. Relationship Between Program Development and Evaluation

Continuum of Emphases

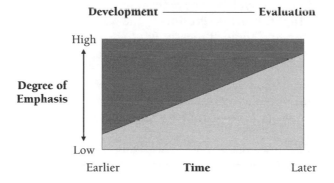

Development ——————— Evaluation

Evaluation Models

Figure 7.1 shows the relationship and continuum between program development and program evaluation. Development and evaluation both occur throughout the life of a program, but the emphasis changes over time. Earlier the emphasis is on the design and creation of the program, development, but over time, as the demands for accountability increase and concerns about program use and impact mount, the emphasis shifts to evaluation. In reality, evaluation is important from the early stages in the design and development of the program, so it is not something considered only at the end of a project.

Evaluation models are typically characterized by the use of a systems approach. An e-portfolio program is embedded in a social system, which may be defined as a structure or organization of an orderly whole, showing the interrelationships of the parts to each other and to the whole (Bertalanffy, 1968; Silvern, 1965). Such a social system may be further described as the parts (for example, staff, users, equipment) working interdependently as well as interactively to accomplish something. The purpose of such a system (for example, an e-portfolio program) is to achieve previously specified performance goals. These system goals can include program objectives and learner outcome objectives (behavioral objectives), which are observable behaviors or performances. The outputs of the system are constantly monitored and evaluated. Information is fed back to the system in a feedback loop, which serves a control function, helping to determine whether the system should grow, shrink, or remain the same. An e-portfolio program will counteract the forces of entropy and remain an open, living social system so long as it engages in meaningful, productive interaction with its environment. If

NEW DIRECTIONS FOR STUDENT SERVICES • DOI: 10.1002/ss

the program fails in this function, it will become a closed system, and the e-portfolio program will be shut down.

There are a number of models that could be used to evaluate an e-portfolio program. We briefly identify and describe several of them that we believe might be useful in this application.

Context, Input, Process, Product. One widely used program evaluation model, Context, Input, Process, Product (CIPP), was described by Stufflebeam and others (1971). The CIPP model specifies four phases:

1. Context evaluation—for example, a review of the history, needs, leadership, and resource assessment; what gaps in services and learner outcomes should be addressed; why the program is needed; and what resources are available to do the work
2. Input evaluation—for example, an evaluation of the resources and materials available for the intervention; state-of-the-art in the field; the availability of successful prototypes or interventions used successfully elsewhere that could be adopted or adopted in the current situation; learner outcome goal statements that could be tailored to the present project
3. Process evaluation—for example, developing prototype programs and pilot-testing them; monitoring the development and implementation of the program
4. Product evaluation—for example, assessing the impact of the program in relation to both its program or process goals, the learner outcome goals, and the context

This model was used in the e-portfolio program evaluation article published in the *NASPA Journal* by Reardon, Lumsden, and Meyer (2005).

CASVE. Lenz, Reardon, Peterson, and Sampson (2001) and Sampson, Reardon, Peterson, and Lenz (2004) described an evaluation model based on cognitive information processing theory that could be applied to the evaluation of e-portfolio programs. This model consists of five phases: communication, analysis, synthesis, valuing, and execution (CASVE).

Communication. The need for an innovation or change derives from several possible situations, each of which involves a need to remove the gap between the existing situation and a more ideal one. The gap may have been identified by a higher-level administrator in the organization, an internal or external task force, the collective wisdom of the current staff, or the felt need of one individual. The agency or organization may have received formal or informal feedback from the users of its services. Whatever the source of this feedback, it typically reflects a desire to improve the situation. There is often not only written information or in some cases hard data; there may also be a certain level of "emotion, energy and motivation to make things better, to reduce the gap between the real and the ideal" (Reardon and Lenz, 1998, p. 208). Examples of questions that might facilitate understanding of the gap:

- Is it reasonable to assume that the gap can be removed? Is this task worth undertaking?
- What is the history of the gap in this setting? How long has it existed?
- Does this gap exist in other places? What has been done in other places to remove it?
- Who in the organization or community is concerned about the gap?
- How do various stakeholders feel about the gap? How much do they want it removed?
- What data are available (for example, survey results, internal reports, accountability studies) with specific information about the nature and extent of the gap?

The information gathered in the process of addressing these questions, along with additional external and internal cues, provides the content that is considered in the analysis phase of this program evaluation model.

Analysis. The analysis phase of the CASVE model requires considering all of the causal elements and circumstances that led to the creation of the gap, along with determining the relationships between the gap and possible solutions. Whether in individual career decision making or organizational program planning, there is too often a rush to the execution phase without careful consideration of all the relevant information and conditions that led to the gap. It is a quick fix to the problem that is sought rather than careful reasoning and a deliberate use of a sound program development and evaluation model. As Peterson, Sampson, and Reardon (1991) noted, "Good problem solvers and decision makers resist the pressure to act impulsively; instead they engage in a period of thoughtful reflection to gain a better understanding of the problem and of their ability to respond" (p. 34). This occurs in the analysis phase of the CASVE cycle when the program leader examines all the relevant information in response to the questions identified in the communication phase.

Synthesis. In the synthesis phase, the question is asked, "What courses of action might solve the problem?" (Peterson, Sampson, and Reardon, 1991). As Reardon and Lenz (1998) noted, this phase asks program developers to "specify solutions that will remove the gap, synthesizing information obtained from Communication and Analysis to identify old and/or new resources and activities to remove gaps" (p. 210). It is at this point that the development of an e-portfolio program clearly begins to emerge as a possible solution to the removal or reduction of the gap.

The synthesis elaboration phase allows divergent thinking, and no options are rejected out-of-hand; this yields the widest possible consideration of alternatives. The program leader or task force working on removing a gap may solicit input in various ways, such as open meetings, focus groups, consulting with colleagues individually, brainstorming, gathering information through internal or external listservs, or posting surveys electronically. A key point to keep in mind when engaging the synthesis phase of program development and evaluation is to carry forward what was learned from the communication and analysis phases. This helps those involved in program development to stay focused on the needs of the individuals being served and the needs of the organization or agency (Reardon and Lenz, 1998).

In the synthesis crystallization phase, the program developer begins to develop a written report, planning document, or proposal outlining the nature of the program intervention being contemplated. This is a critical step in the program development process, because it begins to formulate a strategy for action that can be read, contemplated, discussed, dissected, and criticized by various stakeholders. Quite literally, this written document crystallizes the thinking that has taken place earlier in the CASVE cycle. These need statements or gaps are translated into program goals, which may reflect both intervention process goals and learner outcome goals (Reardon and Lenz, 1998). An example of a process goal is, "Provide access to a e-portfolio tool for showcasing educational, life, and career accomplishments." And an example of a learner outcome goal is, "Non-campus-based learners will be able to develop effective e-portfolios that meet established quality criteria."

Reardon and Lenz (1998) identified key questions to consider during this synthesis crystallization phase of program development and evaluation:

- How might staff roles change if an e-portfolio program is developed?
- Are procedures explained regarding staff selection and training?
- What space and equipment will be needed for the program, if any?
- What resources (for example, technology, funds, staff) are available to remove the gap? Are these resources readily available on site, or do they have to be obtained elsewhere?
- How will the program be introduced to staff and clients?
- How will the proposed program be supervised and managed on a daily basis?
- What are the daily, weekly, monthly, or quarterly time frames for program operation? Will it operate during breaks and holidays? In the evenings or weekends?
- Will there be costs associated with the program? What consultation, technical assistance, and human resource support does the proposed program need? How will these costs be paid, or how will these resources be acquired?
- How will the proposed program change any current procedures? Will some other program be eliminated or curtailed if this new program is added?
- How will the program be evaluated? What special forms and materials, if any, will be needed to evaluate the program? Who will do this? When will they do it? How will clients and staff provide feedback regarding their experiences with the changes in service delivery resulting from implementation of the program?

- Will the information collected by the program and in the evaluation process enable the staff to determine if the original gaps identified in the communication phase have been removed or reduced?
- How and when will information about the success of the program be shared with others, for example, potential future clients, staff, or top administrators? In the larger community? In the profession, for example, through journal articles and conference presentations?

Raising these questions and focusing on possible answers may help in the evaluation and elimination of potential options for the program intervention being contemplated to remove the gap. The ultimate question is whether the program development proposal addresses the causes of the gap identified in the analysis phase.

This list of questions also specifies the kinds of information that a program developer or evaluator might review during the synthesis crystallization phase of the CASVE model. Our professional experience includes painful memories of examples where programs failed because of a lack of careful planning. The close relationship between development and evaluation cannot be overemphasized.

Valuing. In the valuing phase of program evaluation, basic questions about the worth and merit of the proposed program are raised and answered. The basic issue in this phase boils down to this question, "Is this proposed program worth doing given the costs?" A positive response from key persons affected by the proposed program, including supervisory and support staff, the individuals being served, and higher-level administrators, means that the organization wishes to make a commitment to establishing the program as has been proposed, by the program planning task force or the agency head.

In the case of an e-portfolio program, we would hope that the decision to implement the proposed program of new services was right for the administrative unit responsible, the university, all students, and the broader community. A positive response might mean any or all of the following:

- The philosophy of the proposed program is the right one.
- It is more important to do this proposed program than some other one.
- The costs are reasonable.
- The likely outcomes of the program are desirable.
- Most stakeholders favor the proposed program.
- The organization will be more effective in meeting overall goals as a result of implementing the proposed program.

After considering all of the questions and information gathered in the synthesis phase and reflecting on the information obtained in the communication and analysis phases, the program planners and administrators in charge decide to commit to a specific course of action that reflects a consensus about how to proceed and what option or options are likely to produce the desired results. However, any plan about how to proceed is only as effective as the means used to execute the program plan. The next section describes how the execution phase of the CASVE cycle is applied in program development.

Execution. In the execution phase of the CASVE program development and evaluation process, the organization or agency staff takes action steps to implement the program plan or option specified in the valuing phase. It is time to try the program in a real-life setting to see how it works with real individuals (Reardon and Lenz, 1998). This phase is often governed by a specific set of steps and time lines so that all individuals know what is likely to happen and by when. Key tasks are assigned to the individuals involved in program implementation. If one person provided leadership throughout the program development process, that person might continue to provide leadership in directing the implementation of the program in the execution phase of the CASVE cycle, as reflected by his or her revised position description.

Another key element of the execution phase may be a limited tryout with a select group of clients to determine whether the procedures and resources work as expected (Reardon and Lenz, 1998). The activities and services that came out of the program proposal could be pilot-tested with this group. Their experiences and feedback would allow staff to collect information about program procedures and possibly return to an earlier phase of the CASVE cycle to rethink and redesign some of the program activities (Reardon and Lenz, 1998). In some program development and evaluation models, these kinds of activities are described as formative evaluation or process evaluation, for example, "Are we doing things right?"

Communication. Finally, the CASVE approach to program development specifies returning to the communication phase to determine if the gap specified earlier has been removed following the introduction of the new program. Program evaluators are familiar with this general area as product evaluation or outcome evaluation, for example, "Are we doing the right things?" The list of original needs and goals specified in the analysis and synthesis phases is reexamined in the light of data collected in the execution phase to determine if the program is achieving worthwhile goals in a cost-effective way. If it is, the program would likely be described as a successful intervention.

A unique element to the program evaluation process introduced by Lenz, Reardon, Peterson, and Sampson (2001) is the notion of executive processing. When the design and delivery of new programs and services is approached, the collective and individual thinking of staff can play a key role in how successful that process will be. Most readers are aware of how positive thinking contributes to the success of an individual or an organization. This might be reflected in statements such as "We can do this." "We are excited about this new challenge we're facing." In contrast, most of us have also experienced the impact of negative thinking within an organization, reflected in statements like, "We've always done it this way." "What if we try this, spend all this money, and it doesn't work?" "Things are working well the way they are. Why change?" "That's not in my job description." Negative thinking in individuals tends to shut down the problem-solving and decision-making process. The same can be said of negative thinking in organizations. A key aspect of program design and development is to be aware of the potential for negative thinking and to help minimize its impact on the organization's ability to change and develop in order to meet new programmatic needs.

Instructional Systems Design. Thus far, we have explored the logic of a systems view in helping counselors develop more effective programs. Here we focus on how a special application of the systems approach, instructional systems design (ISD), can be used to create a career information delivery system. The systems approach to the design of effective instructional activities has grown rapidly over the past thirty years. Dick and Carey (1985) described a model that may be considered a systems approach because it is composed of interacting components, each having its own input and output, which together produce predetermined outputs. The instructional system also collects information, which is fed back into the system so that the quality of the output can be monitored and evaluated. The ISD model has these steps:

1.0 Identify and prioritize instructional goals.
2.1 Conduct instructional analysis.
2.2 Identify entry characteristics.
3.0 Develop performance objectives.
4.0 Develop outcome standards.
5.0 Develop instructional strategies.
6.0 Develop and select strategies.
7.0 Design and conduct formative evaluation.
8.0 Revise instruction.

Following this eight-step ISD process, the program evaluator designs and conducts summative evaluation. This step is not part of the instructional design process for an e-portfolio system but an evaluation of the effectiveness of the system as a whole.

A Five-Part Evaluation Model. In the cognitive information processing accountability model proposed by Sampson, Reardon, Peterson, and Lenz (2004), the effectiveness of an intervention such as an e-portfolio program depends on (1) a diagnosis of student or organizational (client) needs, (2) a prescription of activities to help address such needs, (3) the documenting of plans and activities that describe the process of intervention, (4) the outputs or primary effects of the intervention, and (5) the outcomes or effects of the primary changes. This model—diagnosis, prescription, process, output, and outcome (DPPOO)—is elaborated in the following sections of this chapter. Basically, the proposed approach is similar to the others described in this chapter. It involves the identification of the skills and knowledge to be acquired in an intervention, the prescribing and documenting of learning activities to help student users achieve them, the measuring of changes in perceptions and cognitions, and finally the determination of whether these changes are manifested in subsequent life-adjustment outcomes.

Diagnosis. In this approach, user problems are defined in terms of needs (Kaufman, 1972), which are the discrepancies or gaps between existing levels and desired levels of knowledge and skill development. The objectives of a student service intervention are derived from the common needs of a group of individuals (Burck and Peterson, 1975). Accountability at the diagnostic stage therefore requires an analysis of student or organizational problems to identify the knowledge and skills needed to solve those problems, a description of the assessment techniques used to ascertain entry-level knowledge and skill performances, documentation of the entry-level performance by the group, and a statement of the desired level of attainment by the group (that is, the objectives for the intervention). The differences between the entry levels of development and the desired levels of development of cognitive skills and knowledge constitute the needs of this cohort group. A cohort group is a group of students with common problems who experience the same service intervention, for example, an e-portfolio.

Prescription. The prescription stage sees the development of a plan for developer and learner activities to meet the diagnosed needs, for example, the knowledge and skill gaps. The development of specified skills and knowledge areas is the objective of a student service intervention; a task analysis (Gagné, 1985) can be used to develop a series of learning activities that lead students from simple to complex skills. The mastery of a content domain, which precedes cognitive skill development, may be structured through content analyses in which students master certain sets of facts, concepts, rules, or operations on which to base higher-order problem-solving skills. For example, cognitive concepts for an e-portfolio intervention might include a knowledge of desired skills (such as communication, leadership, teamwork), the factors associated with the development of such skills, and the ways in which those skills were operationalized in a learning event.

Process. Educational processes are the series of activities, planned and unplanned, that the student performs to bring about change in the diagnosed skill and knowledge gaps. For accountability purposes, it is important to record accurate and detailed descriptions of student activities, the attainment of milestones leading to the acquisition of desired skills and knowledge, the accomplishment of prescribed tasks or experiences, or the quality of the documentation of learning. The most important data to collect are those that indicate progress made toward the development of skills or the mastery of new knowledge, for example, the creation of a portfolio. In the case of developing an e-portfolio program, the documentation of the process could consist of observing and recording the students' use of the system, noting the kinds of questions asked and the need for assistance, user reactions to the results of completing the e-portfolio program, and expert evaluations of system use.

Outputs. The outputs of a successful e-portfolio program are the new skills and knowledge that are acquired, such as the development of computer skills, communication skills, the capacity for reflecting on activities in terms of learning, the ability to formulate feasible courses of action, a clearer understanding of one's own values and the values operating in a social or work environment, and increased planning skills that lead to the successful attainment of self-determined goals. These primary student output changes could be the direct result of successfully using an e-portfolio program. We have discussed the National Career Development Guidelines and Learning Reconsidered as initiatives designed to standardize the specification of student services program outputs. Accountability for output requires documenting the gains made in self-knowledge, problem-solving and decision-making skills, and metacognitions from entry to exit performance levels for a cohort treatment group. These are sometimes referred to as performance indicators.

Outcomes. The outcomes of an intervention, for example, are the effects that result from new cognitive or perceptual capacities (that is, the outputs). These new capacities may include a more focused and organized plan for career preparation; reduced fear of success or failure; a successful life transition; greater satisfaction with a chosen college major; greater job satisfaction or life satisfaction, or both; greater harmony among work, family, and leisure responsibilities; reduced absenteeism from school or work; and increased performance in school or work. Although there are published measures related to these outcomes, for example, the Satisfaction with Life Scale (Diener, Emmons, Larsen, and Griffin, 1985), for most purposes a homemade instrument that is more directly related to the objectives of a given intervention may provide more valid information than a published instrument. The inclusion of open-ended questions may provide the program evaluator with valuable qualitative information about the interven tion as well. Critical incident methods (Flanagan, 1954), in which clients report successes and failures following an intervention, may be especially helpful. In order to assess the enduring effects of an intervention, one-month, six-month, and one-year follow-up studies are recommended.

Inter/National Coalition for Electronic Portfolio Research. This coalition began in 2003 to increase the knowledge of the effects of e-portfolios on student learning and educational outcomes. The goal is to provide leadership in e-portfolio assessment and assemble researchers and practitioners who do work in their own context to disseminate their work locally, nationally, and internationally (Cambridge, 2005). Such initiatives are essential in order to establish e-portfolio standards and learning outcomes and to conduct standardized evaluation of e-portfolios.

Other Models. Finally, we note several other models that might be useful in e-portfolio program evaluations. Hosford and Ryan (1970) described a ten-step model for program development and evaluation using a systems approach. Although their focus was on the development of a school guidance program, the principles would also apply to the development of a student services program in higher education such as an e-portfolio. Sampson (forthcoming) has developed a twelve-step model drawn from his experiences in implementing computer-assisted guidance programs in the United States and abroad. His model has been extensively tested and revised and might be especially suitable in e-portfolio program evaluation.

Conclusion

Most of the evaluation models examined in this chapter are based on a systems approach and employ various qualitative research methods. We believe these qualitative methods, along with the instructional systems design principles, have important utility in e-portfolio evaluation.

References

Ayala, J. I. "Electronic Portfolios for Whom?" *Educause Quarterly,* 2006, no. 1, 12–13.

Batson, T. "The Electronic Portfolio Boom: What's It All About?" *Syllabus,* 2002, *16*(5), 14–17.

Bertalanffy, L. von. *General Systems Theory: Foundation, Development, Applications.* New York: Braziller, 1968.

Burck, H., and Peterson, G. W. "Needed: More Evaluation, Not Research." *Personnel and Guidance Journal,* 1975, *53,* 563–569.

Cambridge, D. "Inter/National Coalition for Electronic Portfolio Research." 2005. Retrieved January 30, 2007, from http://ncepr.org/ncepr/drupal/about.

Council for the Advancement of Standards in Higher Education. *CAS Professional Standards for Higher Education.* (6th ed.) Washington, D.C.: Council for the Advancement of Standards in Higher Education, 2006.

Dick, W., and Carey, L. *The Systematic Design of Instruction.* (2nd ed.) Glenview, Ill.: Scott, Foresman, 1985.

Diener, E., Emmons, R. A., Larsen, R. J., and Griffin, S. "The Satisfaction with Life Scale." *Journal of Personality Assessment,* 1985, *49,* 71–75.

Flanagan, J. C. "The Critical Incident Technique." *Psychological Bulletin,* 1954, *51*(4), 327–358.

Gagné, R. M. *The Conditions of Learning and Theory of Instruction.* (4th ed.) New York: Holt, 1985.

Hosford, R. E., and Ryan, T. A. "Systems Design in the Development of Counseling and Guidance Programs." *Personnel and Guidance Journal,* 1970, *49,* 221–230.

Kaufman, R. *Educational System Planning.* Upper Saddle River, N.J.: Prentice Hall, 1972.

Lenz, J. G., Reardon, R. C., Peterson, G. W., and Sampson, J. P., Jr. "Applying Cognitive Information Processing (CIP) Theory to Career Program Design and Development." In W. Patton and M. McMahon (eds.), *Career Development Programs: Preparation for Life-Long Career Decision Making.* Camberwell, Vic.: Australian Council for Educational Research Press, 2001.

National Association of Colleges and Employers. *NACE Professional Standards for Colleges and Universities.* 2006. Retrieved January 30, 2007, from http://www.naceweb.org/standards/.

National Association of Student Personnel Administrators and American College Personnel Association. *Learning Reconsidered.* Washington, D.C.: National Association of Student Personnel Administrators and American College Personnel Association, 2004.

Peterson, G., Sampson, J., and Reardon, R. *Career Development and Services: A Cognitive Approach.* Pacific Grove, Calif.: Brooks/Cole, 1991.

Reardon, R. C., and Lenz, J. G. *The Self-Directed Search and Related Holland Career Materials: A Practitioner's Guide.* Odessa, Fla.: Psychological Assessment Resources, 1998.

Reardon, R. C., Lenz, J. G., Sampson, J. P., and Peterson, G. W. *Career Development and Planning: A Comprehensive Approach.* Belmont, Calif.: Thomson Brooks/Cole, 2000.

Reardon, R. C., and Lumsden, J. A. "Career Interventions: Facilitating Strategic Academic and Career Planning." In G. L. Kramer and E. D. Peterson (eds.), *Student Academic Services in Higher Education: A Comprehensive Handbook for the Twenty-First Century.* San Francisco: Jossey-Bass, 2003.

Reardon, R., Lumsden, J., and Meyer, K. "Developing an e-Portfolio Program: Providing a Comprehensive Tool for Student Development, Reflection, and Integration." *NASPA Journal,* 2005, 42(3), 368–380.

Sampson, J. P., Jr., Reardon, R. C., Peterson, G. W., and Lenz, J. L. *Career Counseling and Services: A Cognitive Information Processing Approach.* Pacific Grove, Calif.: Wadsworth-Brooks/Cole, 2004.

Sampson, J. S. *Working Smart: A Process for Improving Career Resources and Services.* Tulsa, Okla.: National Career Development Association, forthcoming.

Silvern, L. C. *Systems Engineering of Education: I. Evolution of Systems Thinking in Education.* Los Angeles: Education and Training Consultants, 1965.

Stufflebeam, D. L., and others. *Educational Evaluation and Decision Making in Education.* Itasca, Ill.: Peacock, 1971.

ROBERT C. REARDON *is professor and program director of the Career Center at the Florida State University, Tallahassee.*

SARAH LUCAS HARTLEY *is a coordinator for the Career Center's Career Portfolio at Florida State University, Tallahassee.*

NEW DIRECTIONS FOR STUDENT SERVICES • DOI: 10.1002/ss

8

This chapter provides an overview of the preceding chapters and concluding observations and recommendations.

Concluding Observations and Implications of e-Portfolios for Student Affairs Leadership and Programming

Jon C. Dalton

Technology has received much praise and blame for its uses and influence in higher education over the past twenty-five years. It has been widely praised for its contributions to management efficiencies, information access and analysis, improved communications, and innovative educational applications in colleges and universities. But it has also been blamed for inflated expectations, enormous added costs, depersonalized human contacts and community on campus, and fostering trivial pursuits among college students. There is overstatement no doubt in many of these compliments and complaints, but few today would doubt Bill Gates's claim (Gates, Myhrvold, and Rinearson, 1995) that technology is the one revolution about which we have no real choice.

Few other applications of technology in the higher education setting offer so many possibilities for the reconceptualization and enhancement of career development, student learning, and educational assessment as do e-portfolios. In the preceding chapters, we have examined why and how e-portfolios offer so much potential for deepening student learning and career development in college and providing a more seamless transition from college to career. In this chapter, I conclude with some observations about the implications of e-portfolios for student affairs leadership and practice and some recommendations for future directions.

NEW DIRECTIONS FOR STUDENT SERVICES, no. 119, Fall 2007 © Wiley Periodicals, Inc.
Published online in Wiley InterScience (www.interscience.wiley.com) • DOI: 10.1002/ss.252

The Rapidly Changing Landscape of e-Portfolio Uses in Higher Education

Previous chapters have described the circumstances and motivations that led to the development of early e-portfolio programs and provided several illustrations of how this new digital technology has been implemented in specific higher education settings. Clearly one conclusion that can be drawn is that colleges and universities are still in the early stages of incorporating e-portfolios into institutional programs and exploring new applications. There continues to be much debate and experimentation in higher education regarding the most appropriate institutional forms and uses of e-portfolios, and this flux is reflected in the variety of forms that e-portfolios have taken in different institutional settings.

But while the debate continues about the best ways to harness the potential of e-portfolios, there is also little question that e-portfolios have firmly established their worth as a valuable tool for enhancing student career services, as well as integrating and assessing student learning. Moreover, the use of e-portfolios for so many varied institutional purposes clearly demonstrates the versatility and efficacy of this technology and programming for a wide range of higher education applications.

One should not overlook the fact that students are a major driving force behind the use of e-portfolios in the college setting. As Ceperley and Schmidt (in Chapter Five) and Mobley (in Chapter Six) note, students are increasingly savvy about technology and come to campus expecting their colleges and universities to provide enhanced Web-based technology programs and services. Career development e-portfolio programs are especially popular with prospective students and their parents and have become an important showcase program in collegiate marketing efforts. Lumsden notes in Chapter Four that over forty-five thousand students have used the e-portfolio at the Florida State University, and it is clear that portfolios have become an integral part of student services at this institution. So it is probably not too bold to predict at this early stage that e-portfolios, in one form or other, will be widely used in the future by most colleges and universities.

The Challenges of e-Portfolio Development

Another conclusion to draw from previous chapters is that despite their great promise and early successes in higher education, e-portfolio programs can be risky ventures because of their complexity, cost, and variability. Moreover, as Reardon and Hartley point out in Chapter Seven, the research evidence that supports the long-term effectiveness of e-portfolios is still limited. Furthermore, e-portfolios can be difficult to integrate into existing institutional systems, and their implementation usually requires a substantial investment of staff time, funding, and technical services. There are good reasons for educational leaders to exercise some caution when contemplating the implementation of e-portfolio programs.

One reason that planning for e-portfolio uses can become especially complex is that the process may well involve a fundamental reconceptualization of how an institution defines and assesses learning (see Chapter Seven for Reardon and Hartley's helpful example of how to structure an e-portfolio mission statement around four principles related to learner outcomes). Consequently, it is especially important that educators and administrators have a clear vision of the purposes and uses of any proposed e-portfolio programs before beginning implementation. Goldsmith provides an excellent summary in Chapter Three of specific questions that can help to structure and guide institutional conversations about e-portfolios. I would note too that in order to achieve maximum benefit, e-portfolios must be tailored to the specific goals and circumstances of an institution, and this requires considerable planning and broad institutional collaboration.

Deepening Student Learning and Development in College

One of the most important and far-reaching implications of e-portfolios is their potential to deepen and integrate learning in higher education. In this volume, we have argued that using e-portfolios in ways that encourage students to reflect on their educational development and connect their diverse collegiate experiences with the learning process can greatly enhance student learning and development. The types of activities associated with constructing an e-portfolio require metacognition, which is the process of reflecting on the meaning of what one does and how the various ingredients of one's experiences relate to each other and contribute to one's overall education and development. When students build an e-portfolio, they engage in both a constructive and integrative process in which they not only document what and how they are learning but, more important, are motivated to make sense of what they are learning. This process of internalizing and synthesizing learning is critical to fostering a deeper self-understanding and integration of knowledge.

This kind of learning is deeper since it integrates thinking and experience, intellect and emotion, and makes possible a richer, more holistic learning process. Weigel (2002) argues that deep learning is constructivist in nature; it involves the process of incorporating new knowledge into one's existing knowledge structures. Consequently when students become engaged in identifying and synthesizing their educational gains, they are more likely to do the reflection and reformulation that is so necessary to deeper and more sustained learning. E-portfolios represent an important educational innovation for many reasons, but especially because they provide an easy and versatile means for capturing and assessing a wide range of collegiate educational experiences.

The process of documenting achievements, competencies, and knowledge in ways that demonstrate learning makes students active participants in assessing their own learning and development. Best of all, as Goldsmith argues in Chapter Three, this process gives students an active role in exercising reflective learning. Students do this, she argues, by selecting important learning outcomes, organizing them, connecting them, interpreting them, and personalizing them. Students who engage in this process are more likely to become autonomous learners because they learn to exercise greater control over the process of their own learning. At their best, e-portfolios can help students create a narrative of their own intellectual and personal growth in college, a narrative that helps them see education in the context of their own meaning, purposes, and accomplishments rather than simply as the accumulation of credit hours, majors and minors, and degree requirements.

Opportunities and Challenges for Student Affairs in Creating Powerful Educational Partnerships

Johnson and Rayman observe in Chapter Two that no single area of contemporary higher education is solely responsible for producing student learning and development. The recognition that learning opportunities are pervasive in higher education settings is driving new approaches to understanding how learning is promoted and assessed. When educational outcomes are approached as the sum total of purposeful learning derived from all aspects of an institution's academic and student life programs, it requires educators to consider a wide range of experiences that students encounter in college. Only by approaching learning in a holistic and comprehensive fashion can a college or university fully document and maximize its education impact. The implications of this educational philosophy have particular importance for student services administrators in colleges and universities. This philosophy provides a powerful rationale and strategy for connecting cocurricular student life programs and experiences much more directly to the educational mission of higher education institutions.

E-portfolios offer great promise for creating educational partnerships, but they also pose some challenges for student affairs administrators. Johnson and Rayman suggest that electronic portfolios represent one of the best vehicles for collaboration between academic and student affairs precisely because they provide a conceptual as well as a practical educational model for integrating in-class and out-of-class learning in college. When e-portfolios are used to document and assess learning that incorporates cocurricular experiences, student affairs staff must demonstrate how cocurricular activities do in fact support purposeful learning objectives. And in this regard student affairs administrators have much work to do in developing strategies and techniques for identifying, documenting, and assessing cocurricular learning outcomes. Service-learning and leadership education are two good examples of the types of student cocurriculum educational experiences where considerable progress has been made in documenting and assessing learning outcomes, but much work is needed to demonstrate the educational relevance of other cocurricular educational experiences.

Student Use and Evaluation of e-Portfolios

Reardon and Hartley note in Chapter Seven that little assessment of the effectiveness of e-portfolios use by college students has been done. This is a disturbing finding that should make us cautious in planning and decision making about future uses of e-portfolios. College students generally are savvy about technology and usually determine quite quickly what they find useful or not. We need to understand as fully as possible how students will use e-portfolio programs, what features they will short-cut, what they will embrace, and why they make such critical distinctions. This process of listening to students is especially important when it comes to identifying and documenting educational experiences and learning outcomes.

Another reason for working closely with students in e-portfolio development is that student uses of technology tend to morph into new forms and connections. The enormous popularity of Internet sites such as Facebook and MySpace illustrate how college students can use flexible and creative online programs not only for entertainment and communication purposes but also as outlets for creative expression, opinion, reflection, criticism, and personal accomplishments and aspirations. Students can be indispensable guides in our efforts to develop e-portfolios with educational applications that are comprehensive and effective.

Some Considerations in Considering e-Portfolio Programs

In Chapter One, Garis provides an excellent summary of options or criteria that educators should consider when seeking to develop e-portfolio systems in higher education settings. Garis leaves it to readers to prioritize these decision options, although he acknowledges advantages and disadvantages associated with each set of choices. Since the reasons for using e-portfolios in higher education settings vary by institutional needs and circumstances, it is important to have flexible criteria that can be used to guide decisions based on specific campus goals and purposes.

There are, however, some implicit values in the educational philosophy that underpin the work of student affairs that can help to guide decision making about the development and uses of e-portfolios:

• *Students should be active participants in determining the educational purposes and uses of e-portfolios.* As the primary users or consumers of e-portfolio systems, it is important for students to have an active voice in

NEW DIRECTIONS FOR STUDENT SERVICES • DOI: 10.1002/ss

the development process. Student participation will help to ensure that e-portfolio systems reflect students' needs, interests, and preferences. Student participation is also important from the standpoint of generating support for the substantial resources needed to implement e-portfolio systems.

• *E-portfolio programs designed to enhance student learning should emphasize process as well as product.* The power of e-portfolios to engage students in a process of reflection and self-evaluation of their learning experiences can be one of its most important contributions to student learning and development in higher education. As Goldsmith argues, e-portfolios are a rich tool for teaching, learning, and assessment and can contribute greatly to students' educational development when they are meaningfully engaged and reengaged in creating, evaluating, and reflecting on the contents of their e-portfolios.

• *It may be advantageous to begin with career services when implementing institutional e-portfolios.* It is no accident that the most important early applications of e-portfolios have been in the area of college career services. Here the power and versatility of e-portfolios offer many advantages in documenting and displaying the achievements of college students. Moreover, career services is likely to continue to be a major focus for institutional uses of e-portfolios because of their special appeal to college students, parents, and employers and for the positive role e-portfolios play in college student recruitment and retention. Student affairs will likely always have an important role in e-portfolio development use in higher education because of their traditional responsibility for administering career services on campus.

• *Flexibility for users should be an important feature of the management and control of e-portfolio programs.* System flexibility allows students to use e-portfolios in ways that more directly address their particular needs and interests as well as to become more involved in how portfolio programs are managed. Learning requires interaction and response, and a system that optimizes user flexibility provides a greater likelihood that integrative learning will take place. Flexible use features also give the user more control and investment in the process.

• *Policies for e-portfolio management should promote inclusion and participation by everyone in the academic community.* How institutions construct policies that govern the creation, management, and use of e-portfolio systems has important implications for how effective they are in accommodating critical student differences. Issues such as who pays for e-portfolios, how learning is defined, what roles students and faculty have in the management and evaluation of e-portfolio systems, and the degree to which e-portfolio platforms accommodate school-specific diversity can have important implications for how well the broad needs and interests of students are served.

• *E-portfolios should be introduced to students early in their collegiate experience.* Colleges and universities have made important advances in front-loading information and resources that enable students to increase their competence in becoming self-directed learners. E-portfolios require students to be able to identify, analyze, interpret, and learn from a much broader base of experiences than the traditional curriculum, and this process needs to begin with college entry.

• *Resources allocated for e-portfolios should be sufficient for a complex, costly, and often long-term project.* We have illustrated in previous chapters that e-portfolios can require a substantial investment of resources: money, staff support, training, marketing, and technical services. Moreover, some of the most important payoffs of e-portfolios (such as documenting learning outcomes and developing fully integrated learning-based e-portfolios) require sustained institutional commitment over time and the resources necessary for long-term support.

• *Do not forget to document affective outcomes in e-portfolio development.* E-portfolio systems provide an important educational strategy for documenting and assessing some important affective outcomes that have long been elusive to higher education assessment. Such competencies as ethical integrity, civic engagement, altruism, and social justice have historically been important outcomes of higher education but difficult to assess. This domain of student learning is especially important in the contemporary world because of heightened concerns about citizenship, democracy, and moral character. E-portfolios can provide a way for students to demonstrate learning and development in these affective outcomes.

• *Planning and management processes should include programming content specialists and technical experts.* Communication and coordination among these individuals is especially important in developing effective e-portfolio systems.

Why Student Affairs Leadership Is Needed Now

Garis argues that student affairs needs to assume leadership in the planning, development, implementation, and integration of e-portfolios within the institution. Given the frequent perception that student affairs organizations are not sufficiently connected to the core academic functions of colleges and universities, one could ask why it is so important that student affairs staff provide leadership for such programs. I believe there are several reasons that student affairs' involvement and leadership is critical for the future development of e-portfolios in the higher education setting.

Contemporary research on how students learn in college is placing much greater importance than in the past on the educational significance of out-of-class experiences and influences. Findings from the National Study of Student Engagement (Kuh, 2001), for example, document that college students learn in many settings and through diverse experiences in college. Educators cannot afford to ignore research that indicates that learning outside the classroom in cocurricular settings provides some of the most powerful learning experiences many students have in college. Yet often these experiences are poorly documented, coordinated, and assessed from an educational perspective.

Student affairs staff must also play a leadership role in this process because they are the ones who create and manage most of the cocurricular programs on campus. Student affairs staff have great expertise in understanding the interests and motivations of college students and in creating structures for student participation in campus and community activities. Moreover, student affairs staff are the gatekeepers of student life programs and activities and have easy access to student organizations, clubs, and residences on most campuses.

Finally, student affairs educators bring a holistic philosophy to their work with college students and a dedication to the goal of making higher education a more seamless educational experience. This holistic and integrative approach to student learning is important in the efforts of contemporary colleges and universities to overcome the fragmentation and isolation that often characterizes their educational programs. We think student affairs leadership will be especially important in taking advantage of the important educational opportunities offered by the use of e-portfolios in higher education.

References

Gates, B., Myhrvold, N., and Rinearson, P. *The Road Ahead.* New York: Viking Penguin, 1995.

Kuh, G. D. "What Really Matters to Student Learning: Inside the National Survey of Student Engagement." *Change,* 2001, *33*(3), 10–17, 66.

Weigel, V. B. *Deep Learning for a Digital Age: Technology's Untapped Potential to Enrich Higher Education.* San Francisco: Jossey-Bass, 2002.

JON C. DALTON is associate professor of higher education and director of the Hardee Center for Leadership and Ethics at Florida State University, Tallahassee.

NEW DIRECTIONS FOR STUDENT SERVICES • DOI: 10.1002/ss

INDEX

SS115   **Supporting Graduate and Professional Students**
Melanie J. Guentzel, Becki Elkins Nesheim
Student affairs practice has historically focused on undergraduates and left
support (academic, social, professional) for graduate students to their
respective department or college. But academic departments emphasize
cognitive development of a scholar rather than the psychosocial aspects of
the graduate student experience. This volume focuses on the needs of
graduate and professional students that can be addressed specifically by
student affairs professionals.
ISBN: 0-7879-9057-4

SS114   **Understanding Students in Transition: Trends and Issues**
Frankie Santos Laanan
This volume is designed for practitioners (in student services, teaching, or
administration) seeking to understand the changing realities of today's
diverse, complex college students. It includes recommendations for research,
practice, and policy. The research and practical examples can be applied to
multiple student populations: recent high school graduates, community
college transfers, and older adults returning to education.
ISBN: 0-7879-8679-8

SS113   **Gambling on Campus**
George S. McClellan, Thomas W. Hardy, Jim Caswell
Gambling has become a serious concern on college campuses, fueled by the
surge of online gaming and the national poker craze, and is no longer a
fringe activity. This informative issue includes perspectives from students,
suggestions for research, frameworks for campus policy development, and
case studies of education and intervention. Anyone interested in supporting
student success must be informed about gambling on campus.
ISBN: 0-7879-8597-X

SS112   **Technology in Student Affairs: Supporting Student Learning and Services**
Kevin Kruger
Information technology has helped create a 24/7 self-service way for
students to interact with campus administrative functions, whether they're
on campus or distance learners. And new technologies could move beyond
administrative into student learning and development. This volume is not a
review of current technology in student affairs. Rather, it focuses on how
technology is changing the organization of student affairs, how to use it
effectively, and how lines are blurring between campus-based and distance
learning.
ISBN: 0-7879-8362-4

SS111   **Gender Identity and Sexual Orientation: Research, Policy, and Personal
Perspectives**
Ronni L. Sanlo
Lesbian, gay, bisexual, and transgender people have experienced
homophobia, discrimination, exclusion, and marginalization in the academy,
from subtle to overt. Yet LGBT people have been a vital part of the history of
American higher education. This volume describes current issues, research,
and policies, and it offers ways for institutions to support and foster the
success of LGBT students, faculty, and staff.
ISBN: 0-7879-8328-4

SS110   **Developing Social Justice Allies**
Robert D. Reason, Ellen M. Broido, Tracy L. Davis, Nancy J. Evans
Social justice allies are individuals from dominant groups (for example,
whites, heterosexuals, men) who work to end the oppression of target group
members (people of color, homosexuals, women). Student affairs

professionals have a history of philosophical commitment to social justice, and this volume strives to provide the theoretical foundation and practical strategies to encourage the development of social justice and civil rights allies among students and colleagues.
ISBN: 0-7879-8077-3

SS109   **Serving Native American Students**
Mary Jo Tippeconnic Fox, Shelly C. Lowe, George S. McClellan
The increasing Native American enrollment on campuses nationwide is something to celebrate; however, the retention rate for Native American students is the lowest in higher education, a point of tremendous concern. This volume's authors—most of them Native American—address topics such as enrollment trends, campus experiences, cultural traditions, student services, ignorance about Indian country issues, expectations of tribal leaders and parents, and other challenges and opportunities encountered by Native students.
ISBN: 0-7879-7971-6

SS108   **Using Entertainment Media in Student Affairs Teaching and Practice**
Deanna S. Forney, Tony W. Cawthon
Reaching all students may require going beyond traditional methods, especially in the out-of-classroom environments typical to student affairs. Using films, music, television shows, and popular books can help students learn. This volume—good for both practitioners and educators—shares effective approaches to using entertainment media to facilitate understanding of general student development, multiculturalism, sexual orientation, gender issues, leadership, counseling, and more.
ISBN: 0-7879-7926-0

SS107   **Developing Effective Programs and Services for College Men**
Gar E. Kellom
This volume's aim is to better understand the challenges facing college men, particularly at-risk men. Topics include enrollment, retention, academic performance, women's college perspectives, men's studies perspectives, men's health issues, emotional development, and spirituality. Delivers recommendations and examples about programs and services that improve college men's learning experiences and race, class, and gender awareness.
ISBN: 0-7879-7772-1

SS106   **Serving the Millennial Generation**
Michael D. Coomes, Robert DeBard
Focuses on the next enrollment boom, students born after 1981, known as the Millennial generation. Examines these students' attitudes, beliefs, and behaviors, and makes recommendations to student affairs practitioners for working with them. Discusses historical and cultural influences that shape generations, demographics, teaching and learning patterns of Millennials, and how student affairs can best educate and serve them.
ISBN: 0-7879-7606-7

SS105   **Addressing the Unique Needs of Latino American Students**
Anna M. Ortiz
Explores the experiences of the fast-growing population of Latinos in higher education, and what these students need from student affairs. This volume examines the influence of the Latino family, socioeconomic levels, cultural barriers, and other factors to understand the challenges faced by Latinos. Discusses administration, student groups, community colleges, support programs, cultural identity, Hispanic-Serving Institutions, and more.
ISBN: 0-7879-7479-X

SS104   **Meeting the Needs of African American Women**
Mary F. Howard-Hamilton
Identifies and explores the critical needs for African American women as
students, faculty, and administrators. This volume introduces theoretical
frameworks and practical applications for addressing challenges; discusses
identity and spirituality; explores the importance of programming support in
recruitment and retention; describes the benefits of mentoring; and provides
illuminating case studies of black women's issues in higher education.
ISBN: 0-7879-7280-0

SS103   **Contemporary Financial Issues in Student Affairs**
John H. Schuh
This volume addresses the challenging financial situation facing higher
education and offers creative solutions for student affairs staff. Topics
include the differences between public and private institutions in funding
student activities, how to demonstrate financial accountability to
stakeholders, plus ways to address budget challenges in student unions,
health centers, campus recreation, counseling centers, and student housing.
ISBN: 0-7879-7173-1

SS102   **Meeting the Special Needs of Adult Students**
Deborah Kilgore, Penny J. Rice
This volume examines the ways student services professionals can best help
adult learners. Chapters highlight the specific challenges that adult enrollment
brings to traditional four-year and postgraduate institutions, which are often
focused on the traditional-aged student experience. Explaining that adult
students are typically involved in campus life in different ways than younger
students are, the volume provides student services professionals with good
guidance on serving an ever-growing population.
ISBN: 0-7879-6991-5

SS101   **Planning and Achieving Successful Student Affairs Facilities Projects**
Jerry Price
Provides student affairs professionals with an examination of critical
facilities issues by exploring the experiences of their colleagues. Illustrates
that students' educational experiences are affected by residence halls,
student unions, dining services, recreation and wellness centers, and campus
grounds, and that student affairs professionals make valuable contributions
to the success of campus facility projects. Covers planning, budgeting,
collaboration, and communication through case studies and lessons learned.
ISBN: 0-7879-6847-1

SS100   **Student Affairs and External Relations**
Mary Beth Snyder
Building positive relations with external constituents is as important in
student affairs work as it is in any other university or college division. This
issue is a long-overdue resource of ideas, strategies, and information aimed
at making student affairs leaders more effective in their interactions with
important off-campus partners, supporters, and agencies. Chapter authors
explore the current challenges facing the student services profession as well
as the emerging opportunities worthy of student affairs interest.
ISBN: 0-7879-6342-9

NEW DIRECTIONS FOR STUDENT SERVICES
Order Form
SUBSCRIPTIONS AND SINGLE ISSUES

DISCOUNTED BACK ISSUES:

*Use this form to receive **20% off** all back issues of New Directions for Student Services. All single issues priced at **$22.40** (normally $28.00)*

TITLE	ISSUE NO.	ISBN

*Call **888-378-2537** or see mailing instructions below. When calling, mention the promotional code, JB7ND, to receive your discount.*

SUBSCRIPTIONS: *(1 year, 4 issues)*

☐ New Order   ☐ Renewal

U.S.	☐ Individual: $80	☐ Institutional: $195
Canada/Mexico	☐ Individual: $80	☐ Institutional: $235
All Others	☐ Individual: $104	☐ Institutional: $269

*Call **888-378-2537** or see mailing and pricing instructions below. Online subscriptions are available at www.interscience.wiley.com.*

Copy or detach page and send to:

**John Wiley & Sons, Journals Dept, 5th Floor
989 Market Street, San Francisco, CA 94103-1741**

Order Form can also be faxed to: 888-481-2665

Issue/Subscription Amount: $ _____	**SHIPPING CHARGES:**
Shipping Amount: $ _____	SURFACE Domestic Canadian
(for single issues only—subscription prices include shipping)	First Item $5.00 $6.00
Total Amount: $ _____	Each Add'l Item $3.00 $1.50

(No sales tax for U.S. subscriptions. Canadian residents, add GST for subscription orders. Individual rate subscriptions must be paid by personal check or credit card. Individual rate subscriptions may not be resold as library copies.)

☐ Payment enclosed (U.S. check or money order only. All payments must be in U.S. dollars.)

☐ VISA ☐ MC ☐ Amex # _____ Exp. Date _____

Card Holder Name _____ Card Issue # _____

Signature _____ Day Phone _____

☐ Bill Me (U.S. institutional orders only. Purchase order required.)

Purchase order # _____

Federal Tax ID13559302   GST 89102 8052

Name _____

Address _____

Phone _____ E-mail _____

JB7ND

NEW DIRECTIONS FOR STUDENT SERVICES
IS NOW AVAILABLE ONLINE AT WILEY INTERSCIENCE

What is Wiley InterScience?

Wiley InterScience is the dynamic online content service from John Wiley & Sons delivering the full text of over 300 leading scientific, technical, medical, and professional journals, plus major reference works, the acclaimed *Current Protocols* laboratory manuals, and even the full text of select Wiley print books online.

What are some special features of Wiley InterScience?

Wiley InterScience Alerts is a service that delivers table of contents via e-mail for any journal available on Wiley InterScience as soon as a new issue is published online.
Early View is Wiley's exclusive service presenting individual articles online as soon as they are ready, even before the release of the compiled print issue. These articles are complete, peer-reviewed, and citable.
CrossRef is the innovative multi-publisher reference linking system enabling readers to move seamlessly from a reference in a journal article to the cited publication, typically located on a different server and published by a different publisher.

How can I access Wiley InterScience?

Visit http://www.interscience.wiley.com

Guest Users can browse Wiley InterScience for unrestricted access to journal Tables of Contents and Article Abstracts, or use the powerful search engine.
Registered Users are provided with a *Personal Home Page* to store and manage customized alerts, searches, and links to favorite journals and articles. Additionally, Registered Users can view free Online Sample Issues and preview selected material from major reference works.
Licensed Customers are entitled to access full-text journal articles in PDF, with select journals also offering full-text HTML.

How do I become an Authorized User?

Authorized Users are individuals authorized by a paying Customer to have access to the journals in Wiley InterScience. For example, a university that subscribes to Wiley journals is considered to be the Customer. Faculty, staff and students authorized by the university to have access to those journals in Wiley InterScience are Authorized Users. Users should contact their Library for information on which Wiley journals they have access to in Wiley InterScience.

ASK YOUR INSTITUTION ABOUT WILEY INTERSCIENCE TODAY!